RYA
Dinghy Techniques

Written by Jeremy Evans

Illustrations Pete Galvin

© Jeremy Evans 2011
First Published RYA 2011
Reprinted May 2014
Reprinted February 2016
Reprinted June 2017
Reprinted February 2019

The Royal Yachting Association
RYA House, Ensign Way,
Hamble, Southampton,
Hampshire SO31 4YA

Tel: 02380 604 100
Web: www.rya.org.uk
Follow us on Twitter @RYAPublications or on YouTube
We welcome feedback on our publications at publications@rya.org.uk
You can check content updates for RYA publications at www.rya.org.uk/go/bookschangelog

ISBN 978-1-906435431
RYA Order Code G93

Acknowledgements

Thanks to Steve, Bryony, Dan, Frances, Tom, James and Stevie for sailing the boats with such style and expertise. Thanks also to Cobnor Activities Centre and Hayling Island Sailing Club for help with RIBs and facilites, Martin and Nick from Racing Sailboats, and Alex Ford for his excellent driving.

Photo Credits

Photos by Jeremy Evans.

A CIP record of this book is available from the British Library.

Ring 02380 604 100 for a free copy of our Publications Catalogue.

Sustainable Forests

EMAS
VERIFIED ENVIRONMENTAL MANAGEMENT

Published by **The Royal Yachting Association**
RYA House, Ensign Way, Hamble, Southampton SO31 4YA
Tel: 02380 604 100
Email: publications@rya.org.uk
Web: www.rya.org.uk
© 2011 Royal Yachting Association

Illustrator: Pete Galvin
Cover design: Pete Galvin
Proofreading and index: Alan Thatcher
Typeset: Jude Williams
Printed by: Printed in China through World Print

Contents

Contents

Introduction

Six Dinghies & Seven Experts

For this book we picked six different dinghies, which represent popular sailing categories, and asked seven experts to demonstrate their potential. The aim is to provide tips and solutions for a wide range of sailing aspirations from novice through to hotshot level. Apart from the Laser Radial, which represents the world's most popular dinghy, the five other dinghies are all drawn from the Racing Sailboats range. They reflect typical modern designs, which provide user-friendly sailing, great performance and good value for recreational, high performance and regatta sailors.

Recreational
RS Q'BA and RS Vision suitable for novices and improvers through to intermediate level.

Regatta
Laser Radial and RS200 for improved boat handling techniques that are vital for racing.

High Performance
RS500 and RS700 for skiff-style high speed sailing with asymmetric spinnakers and trapezes.

Steve Cockerill
Single-handed regatta legend, founder of *www.roostersailing.com*. Steve has won multiple international and national championships in the Laser Radial, Europe, RS300, Blaze, Streaker, Graduate and Rooster 8.1.

Bryony Hackett-Evans
Experienced Dinghy Instructor who has worked at Cobnor Activities Centre in England, Minorca Sailing Holidays in Spain, Neilson in Greece and Aquasail in India.

Frances Peters
Hotshot racing helm whose major wins include World Sailing Youth World Championship in 29er class. At the time of producing this book, Frances was racing the RS200 for fun while at university.

Dan Jaspers
Formerly Training Fleet Development Manager with RS Sailing and Bowman and First Mate with the America's Cup Solent Experience, Dan is an experienced dinghy sailor and coach.

James Peters
Younger brother to Frances and an equally hot helm who also won the World Sailing Youth World Championship in 29er class. James moved into the 49er class at the age of 16, with a possible view to the Olympics.

Tom Walker
29er youth squad racer who moved on to the ultra-tippy RS600 skiff combined with crewing Formula 18 catamarans on the European circuit.

Stevie Wilson
European Champion in the 29er, top ranked 49er crew and hotshot helm at the top of the RS800 class, working full time for RS Racing.

The RS Q'BA is a typical modern dinghy, suitable for novices and improvers of all ages, with enough room for an adult or two children to enjoy the thrills of sailing. Its hull is made from rotomoulded plastic, which provides tough, durable construction at the lowest possible cost. The rig is simple with a 2-part aluminium mast and all components designed to fit inside the boat for easy transportation and storage. Popular dinghies with similar characteristics include the Laser Pico, Topper and Topaz.

Sailors: Dan Jaspers & Bryony Hackett–Evans

Conditions: Force 2-4

RIGGING

Whether you arrive with the boat on a roof-rack or trailer, rigging a single-handed dinghy with an unstayed rig is simple and should take little more than 15 minutes.

Roof-rack

Carry the boat deckside down and bows forward on a roof-rack, with the 2-part mast and boom alongside. The launching trolley fits conveniently on top. Other components such as the rudder, daggerboard and sail should be carried inside the car. Use rack straps to secure the boat and trolley to the roof-rack bars, which should be widely spaced to spread the load. After you have driven a short distance at speed, stop and check everything is still tight. At least two adults will be required to lift the boat off the roof-rack, with one at the stern and one at the bows. Slide the boat sideways off the roof-rack, turn the correct way up and lower onto the trolley cradle, which is shaped to fit the hull.

Beautifully balanced with the roof-rack spreading the load and minimal overlap at either end.

Lay the components neatly by the side of the boat before you start rigging.

Components

All the rigging components fit neatly inside the hull for storage: 2-part aluminium mast with halyard, daggerboard, rudder, tiller and tiller extension, mainsail, optional jib, aluminium boom with mainsheet and kicking strap (vang).

Mast

The 2-part mast slides together. Make sure there is no sand or grit at the join. Wash the mast with fresh water to guard against salt water corrosion which could over a long period of time 'bond' the two halves together.

The base of the top section sleeves over the bottom section to form a single mast.

Rudder

The rudder is attached to the transom with two stainless steel pins (pintles) which slide into holes (gudgeons) on brackets. Push the rudder down until a metal plate springs back against the top of the lower bracket, locking the rudder so it cannot fall off if the boat capsizes and inverts.

Top Tip

It is much easier to fit the rudder on dry land. If you do this on the water, the stern will keep moving.

Putting up the mast

The Q'BA mast has a luff groove, which allows the sail to be raised or lowered. As there is no sail attached it makes it really easy to lift the mast vertically. On dinghies such as the Pico, Laser and Topper, the mainsail has a luff tube that slides over the mast. The mast must be raised or lowered with the mainsail attached.

Spread your arms wide to lift the mast onto the boat.

Securing the mast

Lower the base of the mast onto the base fitting (hog) in the forward part of the cockpit. Pulling the mast into the foredeck slot and closing the gate to lock it in position is all that's required to hold the mast up on the Q'BA, which has an unstayed rig without shrouds (side wires). This very simple style of rig works well for recreational sailing, but only provides limited control of sail shape in stronger winds.

Make sure an unstayed mast is securely locked upright.

Pulling up the mainsail

Ensure the bows are pointing into the wind so the boat will not blow over. Unroll the mainsail, locate the top (head) and attach to the halyard. Feed the boltrope into the luff groove and pull the halyard hand-over-hand, ensuring that the boltrope does not jam in the luff groove. Pull the halyard as tight as possible and secure in the cleat by the side of the mast. Coil up excess rope and stow in the halyard pocket inside the sail.

Coil and stow the end of the halyard.

The complete rig

- The boom is attached to the mast with a gooseneck fitting. The outhaul secures the outer corner (clew) of the sail and is also used to tension the foot. The Cunningham secures the inner corner (tack) and is also used to tension the luff and flatten the sail.

- The mainsheet is routed through a block on the bridle line which crosses the transom, a second block on the outer end of the boom, a third block forward on the boom and a fourth block on the cockpit floor, from where the tail end of the sheet is held by the helm. This provides a 2:1 purchase when sheeting in, with the main ratchet block helping to lock the sheet under load.

Test the mainsheet and other rig controls before launching.

- The kicking strap (vang) forms a diagonal link between the mast and boom, with a 2:1 purchase led through a jamming cleat within easy reach of the sailor. The kicking strap or kicker holds down the boom. It is used to maintain sail twist, bending the mast and tensioning the leech. If you are overpowered in moderate to strong winds, increase kicking strap (vang) tension; if you are underpowered, decrease kicking strap tension.

LAUNCHING & LANDING

Don't rush to get your boat in the water. Look around, talk to other sailors, watch them launching and assess potential difficulties to ensure your launching and landing will be trouble free.

Launching

Walk the boat down the slipway. Making sure the rudder blade is locked up, the kicker (vang) and Cunningham are loose and the mainsheet runs free. Keep the bows pointing towards the wind to avoid the boat being blown over. If the wind is blowing across the slipway, you may need to pull and push the boat in a series of diagonal zigzags.

1. When the mainsail is hoisted, you must keep the boat pointing towards the wind.

2. At this stage it's a big help if someone else can grab your trolley.

For the easiest possible launching and landing, always choose a beach with a sideshore wind. Move the boat into knee deep water, pointing away from the beach on a reaching course. Stand at the side, insert the daggerboard and push it halfway down, ensuring the safety leash attaches the top of the board to the boat. Otherwise you could lose the daggerboard in a capsize.

Pull the boat into deep enough water to slide it backwards off the trolley, with the wind blowing onto the bow so it cannot capsize. Hold the boat by its painter or bow. It will be easier if someone can fetch the trolley. If not, you will have to leave the boat by the water's edge, while rushing ashore to push the trolley up the beach!

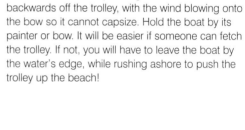

3. Push the daggerboard down until it is below the boom and clear of the kicking strap (vang). Hold the boat side-on to the wind.

Before getting in, lean back and push the rudder blade partly down so you can steer the boat. Step into the cockpit on the windward side and push off with your other foot. Be prepared to move your weight to balance the boat. Grab the mainsheet with your front hand and the tiller extension with your back hand.

4. Heeling to windward helps the boat bear away and accelerate, instead of its natural tendency to turn towards the wind and stop.

Pull in the mainsheet to put some power in the mainsail and accelerate slowly away from the shore. At this point, you will have limited control. The boat will slip sideways and with both the daggerboard and rudder only partly down steering will be very heavy.

5. Look ahead! Watch out for swimmers and other boats.

6. The daggerboard works with a straight push or pull – lean over the top to help it slide through the case.

When you are in deep enough water, let the mainsheet out and, with the wind blowing from the side push the daggerboard all the way down. This is the normal sailing position, though it may be more comfortable to sail with the daggerboard partly up when running or reaching in stronger winds.

Keep the boat side-on to the wind. Heeling slightly to windward will help to keep steering in a straight line, while you lean back and pull the rudder blade all the way down. The Q'BA has a control line on the side of the tiller for this purpose. On some dinghies, you have to push the blade down and lock it with a pin or wing nut, while leaning over the back.

7. Make sure the rudder blade is securely locked fully down. Be aware that the boat will drift sideways while you do this.

Before you sail off, you will need to pull the Cunningham down hard enough to eliminate horizontal creases. Lean forward to give it a tweak and pull some tension on the kicker (vang) at the same time. Make sure the outhaul which controls the foot of the sail is also tensioned. You are now ready to sheet in and start proper sailing.

8. Keep control of the tiller while leaning forward to pull down the Cunningham or kicking strap (vang).

Landing

Be ready for shallow water as you sail back towards the land. Slow down before pulling up the daggerboard and rudder just past halfway. With the rudder blade in this position, steering will be difficult. Let the sail out and heel the boat slightly to windward to make it bear away. Let off the kicker (vang) to reduce power in the sail.

1. Steering will be heavy with the rudder partly raised.

2. Heeling slightly to windward helps prevent the boat turning into wind.

Pull the daggerboard right out before it hits the bottom and lay it in the cockpit. The boat will start slipping sideways and you will have little steerage, so be ready to jump out before hitting the beach.

3. Swing your leg out and step over the side before the bows hit the beach.

Push the tiller away to turn the bows into wind and stop the boat. Swivel round on the side deck to step out of the boat, while holding onto the side at the front of the cockpit.

The water should be just over your knees. If it is much deeper, you may find it difficult to hang on, particularly in a strong wind!

4. Hang on to the boat until it is stable, particularly if there are any waves.

Move to the bows to hold the boat, so that it points into the wind. At this stage you can either pull the boat onto its trolley with the sail up, or drop the sail before getting the trolley, which is likely to be easier on your own since the boat is less likely to blow away.

5. Hold the bows and decide the easiest way to retrieve the boat. Are you going to drop the mainsail on the water or pull the boat up the slipway with the mainsail still hoisted?

Dropping the mainsail on the land

- The Q'BA is made of tough rotomoulded plastic which means it can be left for a few moments at the water's edge with the rudder blade pulled right up. This provides enough time to take off the mainsail.

- First, unclip the outhaul line from the clew of the sail. Then unclip the Cunningham and take the boom off the mast so it can be laid down in the cockpit.

- Pull down on the main halyard to lift it out of the cleat on the side of the mast, then pull the sail straight down so it falls into the cockpit.

- A sail made of laminate such as Mylar® should always be rolled. Never put hard creases in this type of material. Start from the head and roll the sail as tightly as possible, ensuring that the luff forms a hard end to the roll. This is particularly easy if the sail has full length battens. The rolled sail fits neatly inside the cockpit. You may need to use the mainsheet as a temporary lashing to hold the rolls tight.

- Push the trolley down into the water. Then relaunch the boat, slide it onto the cradle and pull up the slipway. The lowered sail makes this much easier on a windy day.

Unhook the outhaul to fully depower the mainsail. Take the boom off the mast and uncleat the main halyard.

Pull the sail down into the cockpit. Remove the halyard and roll from the head.

Pull the boat back into the water to get it on the trolley. Done correctly, it's that simple!

MAKING IT EASY

✓ Check the weather forecast. If the wind strength looks too strong, don't go out.

✓ Choose a spot for launching and landing with a gently shelving beach, which does not get deep close to the shore. You need to be able to easily stand by the side of the boat.

✓ A cross-shore wind direction is ideal, allowing you to sail out and back on a beam reach, this makes everything as easy as possible.

✓ Avoid launching and landing in onshore winds. If the wind is fresh or strong, waves will be driven in and make it difficult to launch and sail away from the land.

✓ Beware of launching in offshore winds. The wind may be light and gusty close to the land, but could get much stronger as you sail away from the shore.

✓ Check if there is any tidal flow. If you are launching in a river or estuary, water will flow at right angles to the land.

✓ Check the difference between high tide and low tide. In some locations, coming ashore at low tide may require dragging the boat across a huge expanse of mud. Coming ashore at high tide may mean landing on a steeply shelving beach, where it's very difficult to stand and hold the boat.

✓ Before you launch, always make sure that any bungs or hatches are secure so that water cannot get inside the hull!

✓ Beware of beach users, swimmers, other water users especially windsurfers when launching or landing.

✓ If the launch area is crowded with boats, wait for them to go. Patience is a virtue for considerate sailors!

SHEETING, TWEAKING & TRIMMING THE BOAT

Mastering the mainsheet, tweaking the sail controls and trimming the boat will ensure you make the most of sailing.

Mastering the mainsheet

- The mainsheet is your accelerator on a beat or reach. Pull it in to make the boat go faster; let it out to slow down.

- Sailing gloves are not necessary for holding the mainsheet, but can make it easier to grip and pull on the kicker (vang) and Cunningham.

- On many modern dinghies the mainsheet is pulled through a ratchet block, which is designed to hold the sheet's load. This allows you to comfortably hand-hold the mainsheet with the sheave engaged, while releasing the load allows the mainsheet to run free. The ratchet is working if it goes 'clickety-click' as you pull in. If not, either the ratchet is turned off (check for a button on the side of the block) or the sheet is led the wrong way round the sheave.

- Some dinghies have a jamming cleat at the exit of the mainsheet block or jamming cleats on each side deck, so you can lock off the mainsheet and don't need to hold it while sailing. This makes it possible to hold the load without a ratchet block, but it will be much slower to trim the mainsheet.

Top Tip

The trick is to be sure that you can flick the sheet out of its jammer in a split second, to prevent the boat heeling over or capsizing in a gust.

Letting out the mainsheet

When you ease the sheet, the sheave of a ratchet block will release, so the mainsheet runs out effortlessly. Do not just let the mainsheet go. Always when sailing upwind or on a reach, keep control, using small arm movements to let out enough mainsheet to sail through gusts without heeling over too far. If bearing away onto a broad reach or run, you may need to let out more than a metre (3 feet) of mainsheet which can run free, with the load on the sheet getting lighter as apparent wind is reduced.

1. Trim the mainsheet and watch the sail. Bryony leads the mainsheet through her back hand (on the tiller) to her front hand, so both hands can be used to sheet in (see page 16).

2. Let out the mainsheet to hold the boat flat in a gust. Dan watches the telltales (see page 16) to ensure perfect sail trim, while checking the water ahead.

Pulling in the mainsheet

Always use the hand-over-hand method to sheet in a centre mainsheet. This will be far quicker and more efficient than the lazy method of using one hand to pull the mainsheet through a jamming cleat.

Hold the tiller extension like a dagger with your back hand and the mainsheet with your front hand. Pull in the sheet, then immediately move it across your body so you can grasp and lock the sheet with your back hand alongside the tiller extension. This allows you to reach down and grab the mainsheet with your front hand, ready to pull another length through the block and transfer it to your back hand. This action could be repeated half a dozen times in quick succession, changing from full out to full in with the mainsheet. Pulling in the mainsheet with swift, fluid movements requires practice, but once accomplished is as easy as riding a bike!

1. Pull in the sheet with your front hand.

2. Lock the sheet on the tiller with your back hand.

3. Reach down to pull in more sheet with your front hand.

Watching telltales

Telltales indicate how air is flowing over the sail. They should stream aft on both sides of the sail. If the windward (near side) telltales lift or droop, it indicates that you need to pull the mainsheet in harder or bear away a few degrees to make them stream. If the leeward (far side) telltales lift or droop, it indicates that you need to ease the mainsheet or head up a few degrees to make them stream.

4. Leeward telltales lift and droop. Head up!

5. Leeward telltales start streaming aft.

The Kicker and the Cunningham

- The kicker (vang) pulls down the boom and tightens the leech, helping to twist the sail so that the top part is depowered when sailing to windward in a strong breeze. The kicker (vang) on the Q'BA can be adjusted while sailing, by leaning forward and tensioning or easing the control line.

- The Cunningham tensions the luff, which helps to bend the mast and flatten the sail, pulling the centre of effort forward to promote easier handling in stronger winds. On a basic boat like the Q'BA, the Cunningham is tensioned before you go sailing. On-water adjustability is possible, but more limited than with a high performance rig.

Pull the kicker (vang) to twist the sail and let power escape from the leech.

Pull the Cunningham to tension the luff and flatten the sail.

How to steer

There are three ways to steer a dinghy:

1. Push or pull the tiller to change the angle of the rudder blade as it cuts through the water.

2. Change the angle of the boat. If you let the boat heel away from the wind (to leeward), it will tend to steer up towards the wind. If you let the boat heel towards the wind (to windward), it will tend to steer away from the wind.

3. Change the angle of the sails. If you pull the mainsheet in, the boat will tend to steer up towards the wind. If you let the mainsheet out, it will be easier to steer away from the wind.

Moving the tiller is fundamental to steering easily and must be used in conjunction with changing the angle of the boat or sails.

- If you push the tiller away and pull in the mainsheet the boat will turn easily towards the wind. If you pull in the mainsheet the boat will turn so far and then stop.

- Letting the boat heel has a similar effect.

- Heeling to leeward encourages the boat to turn towards the wind; heeling to windward prevents the boat turning towards the wind.

Practise steering the boat while keeping the rudder straight. If Dan sheets in, the boat will turn towards the wind. If Dan sheets out, the boat will turn away from the wind with his weight pushing down the windward side.

Heading up towards the wind

Let the boat heel slightly to leeward and use a small rudder movement to change course from a reach to a beat. As the mainsail starts flapping, use the hand-over-hand method to sheet in.

Bryony sheets in hand-over-hand and heels to leeward to turn upwind, with minimal rudder movement.

Bearing away from the wind

- Keep the boat flat, or even better heel slightly to windward, when you bear away (turn away) from the wind. If the boat is heeling to leeward, it will want to turn to windward.

- Pull the tiller to change the rudder angle and ease the mainsheet as the boat bears away, keeping the sail at the correct angle to the wind. If you keep the sail sheeted in, the boat will refuse to bear away, even if you pull hard on the tiller.

- If a fresh breeze, you will need to slide weight back during the bear away. The boat will accelerate as the wind changes direction, driving the bows down which must be counter-balanced.

- Look before you change course. Check there is nothing to leeward behind the sail.

1. The boat may accelerate when you bear away. Slide back to lift the bows.

2. Keep the boat flat and ease the mainsheet during the bear-away.

3. Keep a lookout for boats hidden behind your sail.

4. Heeling to windward with the sheet eased will complete the bear-away.

Top Tip

If you hold onto the mainsail and let the boat heel over...   ...it just won't bear away from the wind!

TRIMMING THE BOAT

For best performance, the boat must be correctly trimmed fore and aft (longitudinally from bow to stern) and sideways (laterally across the deck).

Lateral trim

Pressure on the sail will make the boat naturally heel away from the wind. This has to be counter-balanced by crew weight and sail control. All modern dinghies are designed to perform best when they are sailed virtually upright. This ensures that the daggerboard has maximum effect, the hull shape is most efficient at cutting through the water and the sails provide full power. If the boat heels too far, it will slow down and slip sideways, as well as being very uncomfortable to steer due to excess weather helm.

Look at the angle of the rudder! Bryony has to pull like fury on the tiller to keep sailing straight. The reason? Letting the boat heel over produces extreme weather helm.

Weather helm

The tiller extension should give a slight pull, so that if you let go the boat turns towards the wind. This weather helm provides a balanced feel when steering the boat. But if the tiller pulls heavily, it indicates something is wrong. Either the boat is heeling too far to leeward (away from the wind) or the rudder blade is not locked fully down. If the blade is just a centimetre too far behind the transom, it can completely destroy the pleasure of steering the boat.

The boat is heeling too far, sailing slowly with excess weather helm. Bryony eases the mainsheet to depower the sail and bring the boat more upright.

Hiking

Hiking over the side is the most effective way of holding a boat flat, while driving forwards at full speed. You should be able to hike comfortably over the side with your backside clear of waves. If the straps are adjustable, experiment to find the most comfortable length for your legs.

Lean and look forward when hiking upwind.

Longitudinal trim – bow down or up

Fore and aft trim ensures maximum speed, without bows or stern dragging and slowing the boat down. Dinghies are designed to have maximum buoyancy beneath the rig, which also supports the weight of the crew without pushing the boat down into the water. The crew should normally sit well forward in the cockpit, so the stern will not sink and slow the boat down. But if waves prevent the bows from cutting cleanly through the water, you need to shift the weight back a little. If the boat accelerates on a reach and starts planing – indicated by a flat wake behind the transom – you will also need to shift weight further back in the cockpit.

BEATING TOWARDS THE WIND

If you want to sail towards where the wind is coming from – known as beating to windward or beating upwind – you have to sail or point as close to the wind as possible.

Driving the boat upwind

- A small dinghy with a decent rig should be able to point at about 30° to the wind in the best possible conditions – sailing on flat water with a steady Force 3-4 wind. A light, strong or gusty wind will knock back performance and make it difficult to drive the boat upwind, especially when sailing into waves.

- The trick is to find the right compromise between speed and pointing angle. If you point too high, the boat will begin to stall, coming to a dead stop when you point into the wind. If you point too low, the boat will need to sail a greater distance to your destination upwind.

- The sail is trimmed so that the wind passes over both sides of the sail, with the difference between high pressure on the windward side and low pressure on the leeward side helping to drive the rig and boat forwards. Airflow will not be consistent over the whole sail area. Near the mast, the sail will tend to blow back a little. This indicates more pressure on the leeward side, which is normal when sailing upwind. But if the front of the sail really starts to shake, you must either bear away from the wind or pull the mainsheet in a bit tighter.

- In moderate wind pull the mainsheet in hard so the boom is just off the centreline of the boat. You should aim to sail the boat almost flat. If it heels too far, you need to hike harder over the side. You can also pull down the kicking strap (vang) and Cunningham to bend the mast and flatten the sail so it produces less power, making it easier to drive the boat upwind.

- The daggerboard should be fully down when beating. This will prevent leeway and help drive the boat towards the wind. Use less daggerboard in stronger winds. If the boat feels unbalanced, try pulling it up a bit.

Understanding VMG

Velocity Made Good = true speed to your destination.

- Pointing too low produces slower VMG than pointing a little higher and sailing almost as fast.
- Pointing too high produces slower VMG than pointing a little lower and sailing faster.

Hold the boat upright upwind

If the boat heels too far, it will slow down and slide sideways, due to the side of the hull pushing down in the water. Keep the boat upright by easing the mainsheet to change the sail's angle of attack during gusts, pulling the sheet back in as soon as each gust has passed. Only small arm movements will be required. You can also luff to prevent the boat heeling in a gust, by pushing the tiller away to sail closer to the wind, but this will slow the boat down.

Correct trim from bow to stern

Sit forward when beating upwind. This will lift the stern, reduce drag and push down the bows to extend the waterline length of the boat for increased efficiency to windward. Keep your feet locked together under the footstrap. Only move weight back if the bows start to plough into waves, which will slow the boat right down. If this happens, you will need to bear away a few degrees and ease the mainsheet a little, to keep the boat moving fast.

Holding on

Hold the tiller extension using a dagger grip in front of your body with your back hand. Hold the mainsheet with your front hand.

Always sail upwind with a light feel on the stern. Move weight forward if it drags.

REACHING ACROSS THE WIND

Reaching is sailing with the wind blowing across the boat. This is the fastest and most enjoyable point of sailing when you can really relax and have fun!

Different reaches

- Beam reaching – sailing with the wind blowing at approximately 90° to the boat.

- Close reaching – sailing with the wind blowing from ahead, approximately halfway between a beat and a beam reach.

- Broad reaching – sailing with the wind blowing from behind, approximately halfway between a beam reach and run.

Beam reach – true wind direction is approximately 90ª to the boat.

Apparent Wind

Is most pronounced when sailing at speed on a reach. The primary effect is increased wind speed, producing more pressure in the sail from further ahead of the boat with a tighter wind angle.

- True wind is the wind speed and direction blowing onto a stationary object.

- Apparent wind is wind speed and direction experienced when you are not stationary on the water.

- The apparent wind can change dramatically on a reach. When a gust hits the boat accelerates, which not only increases the power of the apparent wind but also changes the angle so that it blows from further ahead. Be prepared to hike out harder and bear away to the new wind direction.

Apparent wind speed increases with boat speed. The angle of the apparent wind also swings further ahead. This explains why high speed craft such as racing catamarans always appear to have their sails sheeted in tightly.

Daggerboard position

The boat drives forward easily on a reach and you will enjoy fast sailing in moderate or stronger winds. In those conditions, you do not need the daggerboard fully down to prevent the boat slipping sideways. Lifting the daggerboard halfway may make the boat easier to handle, but this is not vital so long as the boat feels nicely balanced.

Dan bears away on a broad reach with the daggerboard half lifted. In Force 2, the apparent wind effect is minimal and the boat slows down.

Hiking and mainsheet

- Hold the tiller extension in front of your body with your back hand, using a dagger grip. Hold the mainsheet with your front hand.

- Keep the boat upright by hiking and trimming the mainsheet. Remember the mainsheet is your power control. Full power is indicated by telltales streaming on both sides of the sail.

- If there is too much power for you to prevent the boat from heeling, pull down harder on the Cunningham and kicker (vang) to flatten and twist the sail to the maximum. If you are still overpowered, ease out the mainsheet or bear away from the wind.

Bryony sails on a close reach, moving her weight back as the boat accelerates. Keep trimming the mainsheet to optimise the effect of gusts, by using a pumping motion.

On a reach hold the boat flat. Watch the telltales and keeping trimming the mainsheet to get maximum airflow across the sail.

Correct trim from bow to stern

Slide along the side deck to trim the boat fore and aft. Your aim is to prevent the stern sinking or the bow burying. As the bow accelerates and picks up speed, slide further aft. At full speed it will be planing (technically when the boat overtakes its bow wave), indicated by a smooth wake behind the stern. The stronger the wind and the faster the speed of the boat, the further aft you will need to sit. But if the boat slows down and comes off the plane, immediately slide your weight forwards to prevent the stern sinking and slowing the boat right down.

RUNNING AWAY FROM THE WIND

Running is sailing with the wind blowing from behind the boat so it is pushing directly against the windward side of the sail. Surprisingly, running tends to be slower and more difficult than reaching.

- Running downwind is the opposite of beating upwind. The big difference is that you can sail at any angle away from the wind, instead of being unable to sail directly towards the wind. Wind hits the back of the sail and pushes the boat along. Unlike beating or reaching, air does not flow over both sides of the sail. Consequently, the sail works less efficiently, with no low pressure on the leeward side to suck it forwards.

- Running dead downwind means the wind angle is exactly aligned with the course of the boat, blowing at 90° to the transom. In reality, it is impossible to run dead downwind for more than a few seconds at a time. Due to the effects of gusts and unsteady water, wind direction will alternate between blowing over the windward and leeward sides of the transom.

Running downwind on a broad reaching course – the wind is blowing from the windward side.

Running dead downwind – wind direction alternates from directly behind and the leeward side.

Running by the lee

If you need to sail directly downwind, it is most efficient to sail by the lee with the wind blowing over the leeward side of the stern. You can sail safely at about 10° by the lee – bearing away further will risk an inadvertent gybe.

Steering downwind

Adjusting the mainsheet and heeling the boat is the most effective way to steer when running downwind. Pull the sheet in and heel the boat to leeward to head up towards the wind; let the sheet out and heel the boat to windward to bear away from the wind. Only small movements of the tiller are required.

Experiment if the boat feels balanced with the rudder up or down. Use body movement to heel to windward or leeward while tweaking the mainsheet to steer downwind.

Trimming the sail

Let the mainsheet out until the sail is almost at right angles to the wind (see the section on Rolling (below)), Ease the Cunningham to put more fullness into the sail. Easing the outhaul will increase fullness in the foot of the sail, but is likely to make minimal difference to your performance, so don't worry if it seems too difficult to grab the outhaul control line.

Apparent Wind

Apparent wind will feel light when you sail downwind, with reduced pressure on the sail. For instance, apparent wind is 10 knots when you sail at 5 knots in a true wind of 15 knots.

Trimming the boat

- Sit near the middle of the cockpit, ready to move your weight inboard if the boat heels to windward. If the bows go down, slide your weight aft. If the stern sinks, slide your weight forward.

- The daggerboard can be retracted halfway for sailing downwind. Do not pull it up so high that the top of the board will catch the kicker when you gybe. If you prefer, simply leave the daggerboard down.

The kicker (vang) helps hold the boom down when there is no vertical mainsheet tension. Experiment with easing the kicker in light winds to put more fullness in the sail. If the boom rides too high, the mainsail will lose power due to twisting.

Don't go rolling downwind

Sailing dead downwind, the boat has no lateral stability and may start rolling. There are various ways to deal with this problem:

1. Experiment with the daggerboard being partly up or fully down.

2. Sheet in the mainsail to about 60°. It may appear most efficient to let the mainsail out at 90°, but this will cause big problems with stability in moderate or stronger winds.

3. If the boat feels unstable and difficult to control, sheet in and head up. With the wind blowing from the side, a broad reach is more stable than a dead run. You can make progress directly downwind by gybing from side to side.

Pull the mainsheet in and head up (push the tiller away) to prevent the boat rolling downwind. Remember that if you are heeling to windward as shown here, the boat will bear away and eventually gybe.

TACKING UPWIND

In order to sail directly towards the wind, you need to follow a series of zigzag tacks.
Basic tacking technique is straightforward, with the boat being turned from tack-to-tack through an angle of about 60°, plenty of practice is required to ensure tacks are fast, fluid and trouble free.

A tack has three stages

1. Turning towards the wind.

2. Head to wind, when the mainsail changes sides.

3. Bearing away from the wind on the new tack.

Steer the boat towards the wind and prepare to change sides.

Duck under the boom and bear away on the new tack.

Use the hand behind your back method to control the tiller.

Turning into wind

Before you tack, make sure the boat is sailing at full speed close to the wind, with the mainsail sheeted right in (1). To start the tack, push the tiller away. This will make the boat spin around its daggerboard, which must be fully down. As the bow turns through the wind, the crew starts moving across the boat to the new side. The mainsheet should be uncleated and eased out a short way, which will help the boat to keep turning.

1. Steer smoothly into the tack with a well powered mainsail.

2. Keep the boat turning through the eye of the wind.

Head to wind

The boat is head to wind when the bows point directly into the true wind direction. Obviously, you can't go anywhere in this position. In order to avoid stalling and eventually being blown backwards, the boat must keep turning smoothly through the dead zone it is facing into the wind (2).

Changing sides

Always face forward when tacking with a centre mainsheet. This enables you to control the mainsheet with your front hand and steer the boat through the tack with your back hand. Pivot your body through 180° (3) as you cross the cockpit.

3. Pushing the tiller extension forward prevents it catching the boom.

Bearing away from the wind

When the sail starts filling on the new tack, push the tiller to the centre position to straighten out on the new course. Pull in the mainsheet (4) as you move across to the new side deck.

4. Sheeting in will help the boat to bear away and accelerate.

Changing hands

You will need to change hands for tiller extension and mainsheet as you change tacks. This is a vital skill for sailing any modern dinghy with a centre mainsheet. Keep practising until you can change hands smoothly and without fumbling on every tack.

- Always use a dagger grip to hold the tiller extension across the front of your body with your back hand. Let your dagger hand slide around the tiller extension, while crossing to the new side. If the extension is long, it may need to be angled forwards to avoid hitting the boom.

- Twist your body round to sit on the new side, holding the tiller extension behind your back with the original hand, while the other hand continues to hold the mainsheet.

- Now is the time to change hands. Move your mainsheet hand backwards to grasp the lower part of the tiller extension. Hold the extension and mainsheet in the same hand, then swivel the extension across the front of your body and grab the mainsheet with your new front hand. If you have problems doing this, sit further forward to provide more room for the tiller extension.

Bearing away on the new tack. Bryony has twisted round to sit on the new side, holding the mainsheet with her back hand and tiller extension with her front hand.

Sheeting in the mainsail pulls her back hand towards the tiller extension, while she steers with her front hand.

Bryony grabs the tiller extension with her back hand, which still controls the mainsheet.

She takes the mainsheet with her front hand and flips the tiller extension over her shoulder, an alternative way to bring it under your arm. With a long tiller extension, you can also try sitting further forward!

Push-pull

If the boat stalls in the head to wind position – known as stuck in irons – use the push-push, pull-pull technique to get out of irons.

1. Push the boom and tiller to backwind the sail and steer the boat backwards until it turns away from being stuck head to wind.

2. Pull the tiller to make the boat bear away and pull in the sheet to power the sail and drive the boat forwards.

GYBING DOWNWIND

Gybing is changing tacks – from starboard to port tack or vice-versa – when you're sailing downwind. Unlike tacking, the wind blows directly onto the mainsail which will power it up during the gybe. This can make gybing a challenging manoeuvre in stronger winds, when any mistake may lead to a capsize.

A gybe has three stages

1. Turning away from the wind.

2. Directly downwind, when the mainsail changes sides.

3. Maintaining control and adjusting course with the mainsail on the new side.

1. Bear away with the mainsheet eased.

2. Tug the mainsheet to help the boom gybe as you steer past dead downwind.

3. Duck under the boom and move to the new side.

4. Centre the rudder on the new gybe.

5. Move onto the side deck while steering downwind.

6. Change over hands and accelerate away.

Turning away from the wind

In light winds, gybing is easy. Start on a reach and bear away by pulling the tiller towards you. Ease the mainsheet until the mainsail is at about 80° to allow the boat to bear away. Try to keep the boat flat throughout the turn. In lighter winds, heeling to windward will help the boat steer into the gybe. Do not let the boat heel to leeward or keep the mainsail sheeted in.

Heeling to windward helps the boat turn into the gybe.

It's critical to time the moment when the boat turns past dead downwind. That's the perfect time to flick the boom across to the new side. Keep steering into the turn until the boom has swung to the new side. If you straighten the rudder too early, too much wind on the mainsail will hold the boom out and prevent it from gybing.

Directly downwind

Continue to steer carefully through the arc of the gybe with the wind blowing from behind. As soon as the wind starts blowing from the new windward side (the starboard side if you've been sailing on port tack), it's time to swing the mainsail across to the new side. On many boats, you can do this by giving the mainsheet a quick tug, or you can grab the falls of the mainsheet, to swing the boom across.

Maintaining control and adjusting course

As soon as the mainsail swings across the cockpit, straighten the tiller to stop the boat turning. The object is to steady the boat and ensure it is not pushed by a blast of wind from the new windward side. The big mistake many helmsmen make is to allow the boat to continue turning, when the boom has swung to the new side. The turn develops its own momentum as the boat spins through 90°, with the crew scrambling to get weight out on the new side and prevent the boat from tipping right over. This frequently results in a capsize.

Straighten your course with the rudder as soon as the boom gybes.

Hold the boat flat in the gybe! If you let it heel, the boat will try to turn towards the new wind direction.

Changing sides

You must steer precisely through the gybe. The technique for crossing the cockpit, while steering the boat, is similar to a tack. Hold the tiller extension with your back hand throughout the gybe, pivoting your body to face forward and swivelling the tiller extension as you cross the cockpit, while holding the mainsheet with your front hand.

Changing hands

Twist your body round to sit on the new windward side deck, with the tiller extension held behind your back so you can keep steering. Use the same technique as a tack to grasp the lower half of the tiller extension with your old sheet hand, flick the tiller extension over your shoulder or under your arm and grasp the mainsheet with your new front hand.

Bryony moves her back hand to the base of the tiller extension, while still holding the mainsheet. She is ready to grab the sheet with her front hand and flick the extension in front of her body.

Board up or down?

Pulling the daggerboard halfway up can help prevent the boat from tripping over its board during the gybe. Make sure the top of the daggerboard is low enough to be clear of the kicking strap (vang) when the mainsail changes sides.

Gybe as fast as you can

When gybing in a strong wind, best advice is not to slow down. The faster the gybe, the lighter the apparent wind blowing against the mainsail, making the boat easier to handle when the boom swings to the new side. The slower the gybe, the stronger the apparent wind blowing against the mainsail, making the boat less forgiving as the boom swings across.

MANAGING A CAPSIZE

All dinghies can capsize, which is part of the fun of sailing. It is important to learn to manage a capsize, ensuring it holds no fear and you are confident of being able to right the boat.

Blown over by the wind

- The most straightforward capsize occurs when the boat is blown over to leeward. This normally happens when you are beating towards the wind, or sailing on a beam reach, and is caused by too much power pushing over the sail.

- You can let the boat heel over to about 45°, beyond which there is a zone of no return, the capsize will be relatively slow and painless. It is easy to prevent this by easing the mainsheet to reduce power in the sail. You also need to hold the boat flat so the end of the boom cannot drag in the water and power up the sail.

Hold it flat! From here the boat will be blown over.

Whoa! Things look a bit hairy with that boom too far out...

Falling in to windward

- Capsizing to windward (the boat falls on top of you) is quicker and more dramatic than a graceful leeward capsize. It typically happens sailing downwind, particularly during a gybe, and is caused by sudden lack of stability.

- If the boat rolls over to windward, pull sharply on the mainsheet to power up the mainsail and stop the roll. If that fails and the boat capsizes, just fall in the water between the boom and deck. The boat may invert (turn upside down), particularly if you try to hang on when you should be falling out of the cockpit into the water.

- If the boat does invert, you need to stand on the underside of the gunwale, hold the daggerboard and lean back to float the mast to the surface, putting the boat at the correct angle for capsize recovery.

1. Oh no! It's the point of no return…

2. Let go or you'll drag the boat upside-down…

3. Relax, smile and enjoy being in the water…

4. Make sure sheets run free and the daggerboard won't fall out…

5. Keep a good hold on the boat as you move round the stern…

6. Stand on the upturned side and float the rig to the surface.

Pulling the boat upright

- Before you pull the boat back upright, make sure the mainsheet will run free.

- Beginner dinghies such as the Q'BA have a righting line attached to each side of the boat, just beneath the gunwale. This saves the effort of pulling down on the daggerboard, which can be strength-sapping.

- Pull down on the righting line or daggerboard to pull the boat back upright, catching the side deck as it drops down towards the water.

- Keep hanging onto the righting line or hold the boat, while moving back to the open transom which provides the easiest and most stable entrance to the cockpit. Pulling yourself up over the windward side requires more physical effort.

Scramble over the transom or windward side.

If the boat has a righting line, use it!

Don't let the boat blow away

- A capsized boat should float on its side with the mainsail lying across the water. Most modern dinghies float high in this position and are consequently blown downwind of the rig, which acts as a kind of sea anchor. The stronger the wind, the quicker the boat will be blown downwind.

- In light winds, this is not a problem. But in stronger winds, you need to ensure the bows are pointing towards the wind before pulling the boat back up from a capsize. If you attempt to pull the boat back up when it is downwind of the rig – wind blowing along the mast and onto the deck – there is a strong chance that the rig will flip through 180° as the boat performs a second capsize.

- The solution is to pull on the righting line or daggerboard and lift the rig just above the water, but no higher. In this position, the rig will cease to work as a sea anchor and allow the bows to pivot towards the wind.

A typical problem! After capsizing to windward, the boom is pointing skywards with wind blowing against the mainsail. Grab the falls of the mainsheet to pull the boom down towards the water, but be careful it doesn't drop onto your head,

BUYING A DINGHY

Single-handed?

The major advantage of a single-handed dinghy is that you don't need to find a crew. The downside is that it can get a little lonely, with no one to share the on water sensation and excitement of sailing. A solution is to sail in company, as a group or racing, so you can share the experiences.

Single-handed dinghies tend to be cheaper, due to having a single sail with less controls. They are usually smaller and lighter, easier to manage on shore, with the extra advantage of car-top transportation.

Popular single-handed dinghies include the Bug, Pico and Laser; RS Tera and Q'BA; Topper, Topaz Uno and Taz. They are all designed to be sailed single-handed, but may have space for a small person to enjoy the ride as a passenger.

The Bug is an innovative, low cost single-hander suitable for children and adults, combining superb stability with surprisingly good performance.

Double-handed?

By design more complex with a rig supporting a mainsail, jib and possibly a spinnaker. It is likely to be a bigger and more expensive boat, as well as being more fiddly and time consuming to set up for sailing. Most double-handed dinghies require a trailer for transportation, which drives up the cost with extras such as under-covers and over-covers providing maximum protection for the boat.

Most double-handed dinghies really do need two crew! You may be able to sail single-handed in light or moderate winds, but performance will be reduced and it may be difficult to launch or land the boat without help. Finding a reliable and enthusiastic crew can be difficult, but the rewards of sailing together are great. Lower performance dinghies are designed to be simple and stable enough to sail with inexperienced crew, although the helm will need to be experienced to maintain control in stronger winds. Larger dinghies may have room for as many as four crew – ideally two adults and two children – and provide a lot of enjoyment for cruising.

Popular double-handed dinghies include the classic Wayfarer; Laser 2000 and Bahia; RS Feva and Vision; Topaz Vibe, Magno, Omega and Xenon.

The Alto is a modern design based on the classic 505, with lightweight hull and sophisticated rig with spinnaker and trapeze for easily managed high performance.

2 Single-Handed Regatta Sailing

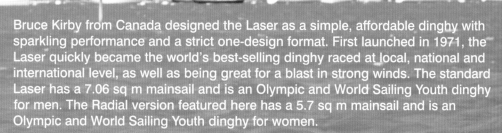

Bruce Kirby from Canada designed the Laser as a simple, affordable dinghy with sparkling performance and a strict one-design format. First launched in 1971, the Laser quickly became the world's best-selling dinghy raced at local, national and international level, as well as being great for a blast in strong winds. The standard Laser has a 7.06 sq m mainsail and is an Olympic and World Sailing Youth dinghy for men. The Radial version featured here has a 5.7 sq m mainsail and is an Olympic and World Sailing Youth dinghy for women.

Sailor: Steve Cockerill – Laser Radial World Masters 4 times and National Champion 8 times. Founder of Rooster Sailing and star of Boat Whisperer DVD films.

Conditions: Force 5-7

ON THE SHORE

Rigging up

A windy session demands respect. No matter that Steve had rigged up a Laser several thousand times in his career, he took a lot of care setting up the Radial for a strong wind session with Force 5-7 gusts out on the water. In such conditions it is critical that everything works and nothing comes undone.

1. Pull the luff tube down over the mast.

2. Attach the boom to the gooseneck.

3. Attach the clew of the sail to the boom outhaul.

4. Attach downhaul to the tack and kicker (vang) to the boom.

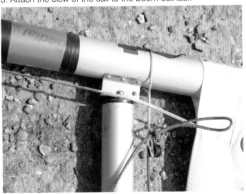
5. Outhaul is connected to the mast for quick adjustment.

6. Lift the complete rig into the boat.

7. Make sure the mainsheet runs clear.

Packing up

No matter how hard the session, your boat and rig will last a lot longer if you take care packing up the boat. Steve always hoses everything thoroughly to get rid of salt residue. He takes the sail off the mast and rolls it carefully from head to foot, as well as removing all control lines from the boat.

Wash off salt residue and grime every time you go sailing.

Wait for the sail to dry before rolling it away.

Steve makes it look easy to carry the complete rig and lift it on or out of the boat. This requires skill and experience, particularly on a windy day! Note how Steve holds the rig so it is directly aligned with the wind vane on top of the building, ensuring he keeps it under total control.

LAUNCHING & LANDING

Launching in an onshore wind

The wind is side-onshore, blowing at an angle onto the beach.

- Before launching, Steve has the mainsail set up with full Cunningham and outhaul tension, plus medium kicker (vang), so he can sail away from the beach without having to fiddle with sail controls.

- The rudder blade is locked down and ready for sailing, slipped under the bridle with the tiller in the cockpit so it can't slide off the deck. The daggerboard handle is next to the foredeck, so Steve can push the board into its case with the safety leash connected.

- Steve pulls the boat bows-first off the trolley, making sure it stays head to wind. At this point you need someone to collect the trolley! He holds the side of the boat to slide the daggerboard halfway into its case, then moves back to quickly drop the rudder onto its pintles, using his body to push the stern and keep the bows pointing upwind.

- Steve holds the stern for a second to let the bows blow offwind, then climbs over the transom while pushing off with his back leg. He moves forward in the cockpit, grabbing the tiller and pulling in the mainsheet to power away from the beach.

1. Steve keeps the boat pointing into wind with daggerboard and rudder ready for immediate use.

2. Steve pushes the daggerboard down halfway, then moves to the stern to attach the rudder.

3. He lets the bows blow round until the boat is on a beam reach, gives a push, climbs over the transom with a hand on the tiller, sheets in and sails away.

Landing in an onshore wind

The wind is side-onshore, blowing at an angle onto the land. The conventional way to slow down and stop the boat would be a complete 180° turn into the wind. This could be very tricky with a strong wind and waves, particularly when you will need to jump into deep water to hold the bows while the rudder hits the ground near to the land. Steve's solution is to undo the knot in the end of the mainsheet and let it run completely out of the blocks, allowing the rig to weathercock and blow downwind, providing minimal power in his final approach to the beach.

Steve lets the mainsheet run out of the blocks. This will let the rig weathercock like a wind vane and completely depower the sail. He uses the outhaul as a temporary sheet when a little bit of power is required, then lets go and pulls the daggerboard out of its case.

Steve lays the daggerboard in the cockpit and uses body movement to steer the boat in the final approach to the land. He jumps over the windward side when it is shallow enough to stand alongside the boat, which is then turned head to wind.

Boat Whisperer

Steve Cockerill has built a reputation as "The Boat Whisperer" featured on Upwind and Downwind DVDs that showcase his talents and expertise in the Laser Radial. Both DVDs provide a huge amount of information on how to manage a single-hander, with practical demonstrations backed up by comprehensive explanations of sailing theory. RYA Order Code: DVD14 and DVD15.

SAILING UPWIND

Beating to windward

• Steve pulls on lots of kicker (vang) and Cunningham for the strong wind. He recommends: Use your back to get maximum luff tension, which will flatten the sail and keep draught forward where it is easiest to manage, while kicker (vang) tension helps to twist the leech and get rid of excess power upwind.

• "Pull the hell out of the mainsheet" by continuously playing it upwind. The object is to hold the boat as flat as possible for maximum control. Unlike many sailors, Steve prefers not to wear gloves because "You get more feel".

• If the water is fairly flat (this session was on protected water inside a harbour) Steve's advice is "Don't use the rudder" because every time you tweak the tiller, it generates a heeling motion which means you have to fight the boat, with increased rocker as the transom and bow lifts out of the water.

• If you are sailing in waves, things are a little different. You have to sail over them (surf), instead of through them which will stop the boat. You therefore use the rudder to sink and lift, using an alternating movement to match the period of the waves. Push the tiller to sink the stern and lift the bows up the wave, pull the tiller to lift the stern and push the bows down the wave.

• What if it's really windy and you're losing control when gusts hit the rig? The safest solution is to let the kicker (vang) go, point 10-15° lower and let half the sail flap, as Steve shows in pic 1. It will be slow but secure!

1

Hike as hard as you can

Adjust footstraps to suit the length of your legs. You must be locked into the boat so you can steer it with your whole body. Pressure on the calf should equal pressure on the leg. If the sailor keeps the inboard end of the hiking pad as close as possible to horizontal, then the outboard end is also more horizontal. This increases leverage and gives more freeboard over the water for flatter, faster sailing, as beautifully shown in this photo.

2.

Tacking in a blow

You may have to ease the kicker (vang) to make the boat easier to tack, since maximum kicker (vang) will hold the rig back during the tack with a very low boom and too much centre of effort over the stern. Try to power the boat round. As you move across to the new deck, kick the side of the cockpit with your front leg to push the bows round. Step across the footstrap with your back leg, which becomes the leading leg as you slip your foot under the strap on the new side. Note how Steve holds the boat virtually flat throughout the tack, steers the boat through a small turn and neutralises the rudder to sheet in and power up in the new direction.

1. Steve has just tacked from starboard to port. He sheets in and swaps hands, with tiller straight and boat beautifully flat.

2. Steve tacks back onto starboard, powering the boat round with full rudder as he ducks under the boom.

3. Steve kicks the side of the cockpit with his front leg as he twists to push the bows offwind. He goes straight out to flatten the boat with the rudder straight.

FINE REACH TO BROAD REACH

Looking for max speed

- When it's windy and you are planing hard, get way back towards the stern to make the boat really take off. For absolute control, the boat should be held flat or even heeled to windward. If you let it heel more than a few degrees to leeward, the rudder will stall.

- Pumping the sheet is a control mechanism on a full bore reach, when any attempt to steer with the rudder will unbalance the boat and slow it down – Steve's advice is, "You cannot fight the wind!" So sheet out to bear away and sheet in to head up, with a few degrees of heel to windward or leeward helping the boat to carve in the right direction.

- Depth in the sail will create drag and slow you down on a fine reach, which requires a flat sail with full Cunningham, kicker (vang) and outhaul tension. But if you are getting speed from catching waves, you will need more fullness to power up the sail.

- Sailing flat out on a broad reach, beware of the boom end catching the water and tripping the boat, particularly in waves. Sheet out to hold the boat flat or heel to windward.

- What about the daggerboard? The Laser dagger is angled well back, so control is all down to the mainsheet. Steve recommends, "If you have time, pull it halfway up. This doesn't make much difference to speed, but will help you turn in waves."

The fine art of catching waves. Steve uses body movement and sheeting to keep the boat at full bore on a broad reach. He lets the boat heel a few degrees to windward (bear way) or leeward (head up), but the boom end never gets close to the water.

Brace and sheet on a fast reach. Look where you're going and keep the tiller straight.

Bearing away in a gust with confused waves. The boom end is as close as it wants to get!

The thrill of power. Steve leans right back and accelerates onto a broad reach. Note that the rudder stays straight!

Is your sail happy or unhappy?

A happy sail is perpendicular to the wind and will let the boat sail sweetly. If you set the sail in an unhappy position, the boat will want to make it happy by turning in a different direction. It's a waste of effort trying to fight this natural reaction.

Lying abeam

What happens if you just want to sit there?
To avoid getting stuck in irons, pull on the boom, pull up the centreboard and let off kicker (vang) which will keep draught forwards and prevent the boat turning into wind.

Heading up onto a beat

When changing course from a broad reach to a beat a few degrees of leeward heel are enough to let the bows pivot towards the wind. Steve pulls in the flapping mainsail hand-over-hand, reaching right back over his shoulder to pull in as much sheet as possible, with a final tweak to get the sail set in the 'happy' position on the new course. Look at the tiller (2). It is dead straight throughout the manoeuvre. The rudder doesn't move at all. If it does, the stern will lift and speed will fall.

1.
2.

Steve heads up onto a beat in the middle of a 30 knot gust. The combination of rudder movement and strong wind drives down the stern and lifts the bow as the boat turns towards the wind. Steve goes for it hand over hand, pulling a metre of mainsheet past his head until it is hard in, then settles down for a hard beat.

3.
4.

Bearing away onto a run

The key to bearing away is let the sail out and allow the boat to heel to windward. Be aware that the rudder provides a lifting mechanism which will lift the transom and sink the bow.

1. Release mainsheet.

2. Move in smartly.

3. Use the rudder to finish the bear-away and drop the boom back down parallel to the water.

1. Heeling to windward with mainsheet eased guarantees a clean bear-away.

2 & 3. Steve moves in and uses the rudder to complete the bear-away, lifting the transom and sinking the bows while trimming the mainsheet.

The Wind Knows Best!

There are some occasions when you just have to go with the wind. Hit by a master blaster, Steve switches to temporary survival mode.

SAILING DOWNWIND

From deep downwind to by-the-lee

- The sail needs to be well out when sailing deep downwind, with kicker (vang) tension to hold down the boom and Cunningham eased to put some fullness in the sail.

- Mainsheet and trim are primary controls for steering downwind. When a gust hits the leech will be blown open. Sheeting in 15cm (6 inches) as the boat bears away on apparent wind, will recover the leech and restore a happy feeling in the sail. If the boat rolls to windward, tweak in the sheet to stop the bear-away and get back to level sailing.

- If you head really deep downwind, you will start sailing by the lee. This is clearly indicated when the telltales start reversing. Everything now goes into reverse, since the wind is now blowing onto the sail from the leeward side. If you need to power up, let out the mainsheet. If you want to depower, pull in the mainsheet. The point of maximum balance is when the centre of effort in the sail is right over the daggerboard.

Starboard tack deep downhill – kicker (vang) on and Cunningham eased. Port tack dead downwind in waves.

Steve tweaks the mainsheet to hold the leech as he bears away on apparent wind.

By the lee changes the situation. Mainsheet in to depower; mainsheet out to power up.

Relax and keep the tiller straight!

Try to keep the main power area of the sail right over the daggerboard for maximum balance.

Gybing in a blow

Steve makes a Force 6 gybe look easy, which is the result of more than twenty years of Laser competition with multiple victories in the Radial class. Note how he keeps the boat almost flat throughout the turn. On the approach, he looks ahead to the exact spot for the gybe. The sail is in a happy position and the boat at full bore. A slight heel to windward helps the turn, flattening the transom and lifting the bow, as Steve reverses the tiller to steer into the gybe and ducks his upper body towards the new side. The speed of the boat keeps the sail light as it flicks across, when Steve applies a touch of reverse rudder to stop the turn and keep the arc of the gybe small, ensuring the transition is from deep downwind to deep downwind.

Steve looks where he's going, with slight heel to windward as he turns into the gybe with the tiller extension reversed.

Swinging dead downwind with the bows lifted as Steve ducks to the new side.

Sailing fast reduces apparent wind as the mainsail gybes, with Steve reversing the rudder to cut the arc of the turn and make a safe exit deep downwind.

THE CAPSIZE SOLUTION

San Francisco Roll

If it's blowing Force 4 or more, Steve recommends the San Francisco Roll. It's very difficult to pull the boat up from a capsize in a strong wind without problems, since the hull gets quickly blown downwind of the rig. The result is that by the time you've pulled the rig upright, you are on the leeward side of the boat. Bang! The wind hits the wrong side of the sail and the boat capsizes on top of you, having pirouetted from capsize to capsize in a 180° roll. So you start to pull the boat upright for a second time, but by the time the rig lifts off the water it's once again on the windward side. Bang! Another 180° roll!

1. The boat has blown downwind of the rig.

One solution could be to swim the bow round until the boat is facing into wind, but that is truly strength sapping and leaves enough time for the boat to drift downwind again. The San Francisco Roll overcomes all these problems with one dynamic movement, which capitalises on the boat's natural inclination to roll through 180°.

1. You can see Steve standing on the underside of the gunwale and holding onto the daggerboard. The Laser is floating high on its side and the rig is partly sunk, as he is pulling the boat up from a full inversion. The buoyant hull has blown downwind of the rig, which acts as a sea anchor. The wind is blowing from right to left, straight into Steve's face.

2. If you try to pull it up, the boat will flip right over.

2. Steve makes sure the daggerboard is pulled right out and pushes up the self-bailers. He doesn't want to get stubbed, slashed or trapped on his journey under the boat!

3. Next stage is lean back to lift the rig out of the water, just as in a normal capsize recovery. But as soon as wind gets under the rig, Steve pushes down hard on the daggerboard and holds on tight with both hands.

3. Steve hangs onto the daggerboard and takes a 180° ride!

4. Whoosh! The rig lifts all the way out of the water with Steve providing a pendulum weight underneath and the full force of the wind hitting the windward side of the sail. The inevitable 180° roll is fast and powerful enough to pull Steve right under the boat, before he emerges spluttering on the windward side, still holding the daggerboard.

5. Having completed the roll, Steve is perfectly placed to pull the boat upright with the rig lying downwind. It's then easy to clamber in over the windward side.

> **Practice is required to get this manoeuvre sorted!**

4. The boat flips over and takes Steve with it.

5. Steve comes up for air as the Laser blows over to leeward.

6. He grabs the daggerboard tip on the windward side.

7. Then pulls himself up…

8. … and rights the Laser.

9. The Laser is in a perfect beam reach position.

10. Roll and retrieval takes little more than a minute!

A single-handed skiff, fitted with trapeze and spinnaker, provides a unique sailing experience in a fresh breeze. Thrilling performance relies on very good technique – lots of practice is required to manage this level of high performance, but the rewards are immense.

Sailor: Tom Walker – 29er, RS600, Formula 18

Conditions: Force 3-4

"The overall key to enjoying these boats is not to fight against them. Always make your actions firm and decisive. If you believe you are going to get through that gybe, then you will succeed!"

LAUNCHING & LANDING

Things can easily go wrong when launching or landing a high performance single-hander. Specific issues to consider include:

1. The boat is very light and quite unstable, so will blow over easily. You need help with the trolley.

2. Too much power in the rig. The mainsail must be fully depowered with Cunningham and kicker (vang) let right off. Check the mainsheet will run free.

3. Boat stability. Hold the boat by the forward part of the windward rack. This will control where it's pointing and also provide maximum leverage to keep the rig upright. Holding this type of boat by the forestay is not an option!

Tom launches the RS700 at Hayling Island SC in an offshore wind.

He holds the rack and spins the boat onto a beam reach.

Being super-slim, Tom opts to step up inside the rack, others will use the open stern.

Stand to sail a skiff, unless you are out on the wire.

Good balance is required until the daggerboard and rudder are fully down.

- **How do you get on board?** Tom has a neat solution, climbing between the racks, which are at their widest setting for a lightweight sailor. A more usual solution is to pivot the boat onto a beam reaching course from behind the windward rack and step through the open transom, pushing off with your back leg.

- **How do you sail away from the beach?** Keeping your weight to windward is a key solution, making the boat bear away, which gives it some power, speed and steerage. If you jump on and stand on the centreline or leeward side, the boat will want to pivot into the wind and end up in irons after just a few metres. In almost any wind direction this will put you back on the beach, minus your dignity!

- Before leaving the beach, make sure you put the daggerboard in with at least some foil depth under the hull. This adds stability and means you only have to use one hand, or perhaps a foot, to push the rest of the board down.

- High performance single-handers such as the RS700, RS600 and Musto Skiff have deep daggerboards with fragile tips, which should never be allowed to hit the bottom. Stand over the daggerboard to get a direct pull when retracting the board.

Chris Aston launches his RS700 from Weston SC on Southampton Water. With wind cross-offshore, he steps onto the transom and pushes off with his back foot to get away from the beach.

SAILING UPWIND

Sail free

A high performance boat like the RS700 is designed to plane upwind in winds over 12-15 knots. Bear away to sail fast and free with maximum power in the rig and full leverage on the trapeze to optimise VMG. Do not attempt to pinch upwind which will stall the boat and slow it down.

Trimming the mainsheet

The mainsail on the RS700 is not designed to be sheeted to the centreline. The end of the boom meets the back of the leeward rack, providing the correct angle of attack for sailing upwind on a fine reach. The mainsheet has a central jammer for use downwind, but should be hand-held for instant response to gusts when sailing upwind.

Flat wiring

Powering upwind at the top end of Force 3, Tom stands with the balls of his feet together at the front of the rack, flat-wiring for maximum leverage. Stand tall in your harness and keep your shoulders back! Don't 'sit up' unless under-powered.

Hold the rig upright

Tom keeps the boat heeling very slightly to windward. If a gust hits, the boat will be lifted to the upright position – not to leeward, which would make it slip sideways and pivot into wind. In stronger winds or waves, Tom would move aft, pulling down more Cunningham tension to flatten the sail with increased kicker (vang) to twist open the leech.

How high on the wire?

Trapeze height should be as low as possible for maximum leverage with enough height to keep above waves. To adjust the height, Tom transfers the mainsheet to his back hand, which is holding the tiller, using his free front hand to tweak the trapeze up or down.

Ducking under the boom

The clew of the RS700 is cut high, providing enough space for the crew to cross under the boom during tacks and gybes. With the centre of effort well aft and no jib to pull the bows round, a successful tack requires commitment. Beware of too much kicker (vang) tension which can stall the boat head-to-wind. A good pre-tack tip is to pull yourself up on the trapeze a few centimetres on the new tack side. This makes it easier to hook-on, without the risk of going out and flat-wiring on the new side, which can easily lead to a dunking if you are not fully powered up on the new tack.

Tacking on the wire

1. Tom moves his front hand onto the trapeze handle, holding the mainsheet and supporting his weight as he steers into the tack.

2. As the bows turn through the wind, Tom pulls himself upright and stands on the rack. Avoid sitting down on the side as you come in, this makes the tack slower. Also you're less able to react to gusts and other unforeseen dangers from a static sitting position.

3. Tom steps into the cockpit, letting go of the trapeze handle and easing the mainsheet to prevent the boat stalling midway through the tack. He immediately ducks under the boom with the bows just passing head to wind, facing forward and kneeling on his front leg. Note that the boat has stayed almost level throughout the manoeuvre, with only light kicker (vang) tension so the mainsail can depower while the boat turns.

4. Tom pivots to the new side, still holding the tiller extension with his original back hand and mainsheet with his original front hand. Lifting the low bow off the water helps the boat to tack round.

5. Tom steps onto the new side deck and pivots round, making the change-over between tiller and sheet hands.

6. With one fluid movement, Tom grabs the trapeze handle, steps onto the rack with his front foot and bears away to power up the mainsail. Holding the trapeze handle and mainsheet with his front hand, Tom goes out on the rack and automatically pulls in the mainsheet with this movement, clipping on as he powers up on the new tack.

1. Tom grabs the trapeze wire handle to take his weight.

2. He pulls himself up and stands on the rack as the bows turn into wind.

3. He steps into the cockpit, pivoting round to face forward while ducking under the boom.

4. Tom moves to the new side while pivoting round, with tiller and mainsheet reversed in normal dinghy tack style.

5. He steps out on the rack as the boat bears away on the new tack.

6. Tom grabs the trapeze ring, ready to hook in, sheet in and go out on the wire.

Bearing away downwind

Tom lets the boat heel to windward, which uses the natural curve of the hull to help the bear-way, with minimum use of the rudder and therefore minimum drag. A careful balancing act is required to stay on the wire, trimming the mainsheet to keep maximum power in the rig as the apparent wind changes, while stepping back on the rack to let the bows fly as the boat accelerates onto a beam reach.

Easing the mainsheet and bearing away is not so easy. Heeling to windward helps the boat bear away, but the last thing you want is to be dumped to windward on the trapeze, which rapidly leads to a point of no return with the boat falling on top of you. Tom uses precise mainsheet control to maintain enough lift to stay on the wire, stepping back on the rack as the boat accelerates offwind.

SAILING DOWNWIND

The speed of a boat alters the angle of the apparent wind. As the boat accelerates, the apparent wind swings forward so it blows from further ahead. This phenomenon is most obvious on windsurfers, catamarans and skiff-style dinghies like the RS700, which appear to have their sails sheeted in tight when there is a good breeze. High boat speed ensures the apparent wind angle swings onto the bows, even when sailing downwind.

Hoists and drops

Tom stands in the middle of the cockpit, steers deep downwind and gives a few pulls on the handle to hoist or lower the RS700 spinnaker, which has a multi-purchase pump system. The advantage of the pump system is that one hand is free to steer the boat. The disadvantage is that it has more friction and is a little slower than a conventional spinnaker halyard and retrieval system, as used on the similar Musto Skiff.

Follow the kite

- Once the spinnaker is up, Tom tensions and cleats the mainsheet, which is trimmed to the apparent wind and will provide a backstay for the spinnaker. He steps out onto the rack, sheeting in the spinnaker and heading up to build the apparent wind.

- Bear away and let the kite follow the apparent wind with every gust. If you let the boat heel too far to leeward, control will get progressively more difficult as it automatically tries to turn upwind, putting increased side force on the mainsail.

Trapeze off the side of the boat, before going right out with the kite.

Step right out when you feel relaxed and stable.

Bear away on gusts to stay flat and prevent the leeward rack burying.

Perfect trim in all directions – time to look at the camera!

Flat and fast

Perfect trim with the boat sailing flat and fast on a light wind gust. Tom is standing near the back of the rack, looking ahead to read the water with his front leg braced and back leg bent against the forward pull of the trapeze wire. The spinnaker is curling on the leading edge, providing maximum power.

Gybing on the wire

Keeping speed throughout the gybe is key to the manoeuvre and can compensate for bad kite trim or wobbly steering. Although it goes against your natural instincts to initiate the gybe when sailing at full speed, this helps keep the full strength of the wind off the mainsail, due to the diminished apparent wind. If speed is carried into the gybe, the middle stage of the gybe can be taken relatively slowly as momentum should help to carry you through. An important trick is to ease the mainsheet prior to the gybe, which makes the whole gybing process a lot easier.

Bear away and step in as the windward rack goes down.

Duck under the boom with mainsheet eased, while holding the old spinnaker sheet.

Tom bears away with the mainsheet eased for the gybe. He stands up and steps off as the windward rack goes down, helping the boat pivot through the wind. Note that very little rudder movement is needed to turn the boat. Tom flicks the tiller extension across to the new side and dips beneath the boom as it swings across the cockpit, with the boat sailing deep downwind.

Sheet in the spinnaker on the new side as the boat turns through the wind.

Use trim to help steer the boat while staying downwind.

Tom locks the tiller extension against the new windward rack to hold the rudder straight and keep the boat heading downwind. The old spinnaker sheet should be under tension to prevent the loose kite from blowing around the luff, creating a twist when Tom sheets in on the new side.

Move onto the rack, turning towards the wind and sheeting in.

Hook on, build up power and sheet in the mainsail before going out on the wire.

Tom moves out onto the rack and tweaks in the spinnaker sheet, heading up to build apparent wind on the new course.

Before you go into a gybe, bear away and get the boat sailing flat at full speed to reduce apparent wind power on the mainsail.

Whoa!

It is good to give the boat a slight angle of windward heel going into the gybe to help with the bear-away. Too much windward heel will make the boat pivot too quickly and push the rack underwater, a state of affairs that is unlikely to end well!

Enjoy the swim

There is no worse feeling for a skiff sailor than stalling mid-gybe. The mainsail powers up with a blast of apparent wind which fires the boom across the cockpit. If this happens, the best course of action is:

1. Keep your head down.

2. Enjoy the swim.

3. Try to learn from your mistakes!

CAPSIZE RETRIEVAL

Mind the gap

The gap between rack and gunwale provides Tom in his RS700 with an ideal route between daggerboard and cockpit. If that's not available, the best route is likely to be round the front of the rack, which also provides a great hand-hold for pulling the boat upright. If you drop into the water, beware that the RS700 daggerboard has a disconcertingly sharp trailing edge and may be difficult to grab if the high-floating hull starts to invert.

These boats invert easily. get onto the daggerboard as quickly as possible.

Make sure the mainsheet is uncleated and haul the spinnaker back inside its chute.

Take a breather before the next stage.

Pull on the rack to lift the rig and right the boat. If you cannot fit between the rack and the boat, get on board via the transom.

Lifting the rig

If the hull swings downwind of the rig, you get the normal problem of being on the wrong side when the rig lifts off the water. Theoretically you could swim to the bow and pull it into wind, but this is a slow and strength-sapping solution.

Tom's first choice would be a San Francisco Roll (pages 50-51), but you need a Force 4 to make it work and a bigger sailor may find it difficult to manage with racks on each side of the boat. An alternative method is based on Tom's experience with the ultra-tippy RS600. This requires agility, good timing and the kind of practice that comes with hundreds of capsize recoveries!

1. Put your back leg onto the daggerboard and your front leg over the deck in front of the rack, possibly resting on the mast base.
2. Lean your body weight back, pulling against the rack to lift the masthead out of the water.
3. When the sail lifts, push your back foot off the daggerboard.
4. As the boat comes upright, step in front of the mast and onto the new windward side, grabbing the shroud to counter-balance the flick of the boat as it tries to capsize in the other direction.

Alternatively, you could just let the boat capsize over on top of you, duck under the rack or swim round the back and get on the daggerboard quickly before it turtles.

The easiest possibility is to lift the masthead out of the water a fraction, but not enough to right the boat. If you are lucky, the wind gets under the head and blows the rig back downwind of the hull, which is exactly where you want it to be!

The RS Vision is an entry-level dinghy, which combines stability and easy handling in light or moderate winds with exciting performance in a blow. It's designed to be sailed by two crew with mainsail and jib, plus the options of using a spinnaker and trapeze as technique improves. The hull is made from tough, durable rotomoulded plastic construction, with an aluminium mast supported by wire forestay and shrouds. There is a wide choice of rotomoulded dinghies with similar characteristics, including the Laser Bahia and Topaz Xenon.

Helm: Dan Jaspers

Crew: Bryony Hackett–Evans

Conditions: Force 2-4

RIGGING TIPS

Basic principles for rigging a twin-crew dinghy with shrouds holding up the rig will always be much the same. However, there may be many small differences in the rigging procedure and different ways of putting things together can work equally well. If your dinghy has a rigging manual, best advice is use it as your guide. If not, stick to basic principles and work out your own methods for making the rig work well. Never rush to get on the water. Allow at least half an hour to rig up with mainsail and jib, plus another half hour if you wish to rig a spinnaker.

The mainsail

Choose an open space for rigging where you won't be in anyone's way.

When rigging, the boat should be sitting snugly on its trailer with bows pointing into the wind. The mast is supported by two wire shrouds and a temporary rope forestay which is removed when the jib is fully rigged. Unroll the mainsail inside the cockpit, with the luff by the mast. Check the battens are in position and under tension before hoisting the sail.

1. Make a loop in the top of the halyard and push it through the cringle (eye) at the head of the mainsail. Fold the loop over the ball to lock the halyard in position.

Different dinghies have various methods of attaching halyard. The plastic ball shown here is simple and secure.

2. Insert the head of the mainsail into the luff groove in the mast. It may be necessary to have one person pulling on the halyard and one person guiding the bolt rope into the luff groove as the mainsail is pulled up the mast. Secure the halyard to its cleat when the head of the sail is right at the top of the mast.

 If the bolt rope jams as you pull the sail up the mast, get someone to feed it into the groove.

Pull hard on the downhaul (Cunningham) control line to tension the luff. This will bend the mast and flatten the sail, making the mainsail easier to handle in fresh winds.

4. The clew of the mainsail is attached to the boom groove by a plastic slider. An outhaul control line is used to adjust foot tension.

The Gnav shown here is an aluminium strut between mast and boom. The boom connector slides forward or back. Pulling the Gnav forward holds the boom down when the mainsheet is eased.

Reefing lines

Like other recreational dinghies, the size of a Vision mainsail can be reduced on shore or on the water. The slab reefing system has reefing lines led to cringles at the same height on the leech and luff of the sail. A single control line at the front of the boom pulls the two reefing lines down together, effectively removing a slab from the sail which can be rolled neatly alongside the boom.

Dan sets up reefing lines, which are used to pull down the leech of the mainsail, with corresponding reefing lines used to pull down the luff.

3. A multi-purchase downhaul control line or Cunningham (invented by the American sailor Briggs Cunningham) is attached to a cringle near the tack. This is used to adjust luff tension and is of major importance for depowering the sail in stronger winds.

Tensioning the outhaul flattens the foot of the mainsail.

Gnav or kicking strap (vang)?

Many modern dinghies are fitted with an aluminium strut known as a gnav (reverse vang) which forms a triangle with the mast above the boom. The end of the gnav slides along a short track on top of the boom and is adjusted with a control line. Pulling the gnav forward pushes the boom down, which can be used to increase power in the sail. Letting the gnav slide back lets the boom ride up, which can be used to decrease power in the sail. The classic alternative to a gnav is a multi-purchase kicking strap (vang) which forms a triangle with the mast below the boom. The principal advantage of the gnav is that it leaves a clear space for the crew in the front of the cockpit.

The Jib

1. The head of the jib is attached to a swivel on the halyard. The tack of the jib is attached to a swivel on the bar behind the spinnaker chute. A layer of tape will help to ensure the pins which hold these vital connections together cannot come undone.

2. Most recreational dinghies are fitted with a furling jib. Pull the control line in the cockpit to roll the jib like an umbrella; uncleat the control line and pull the sheets to unroll the jib.

3. Use a loop knot to attach the sheet to the cringle in the clew of the jib. Tie the ends together to provide a continuous sheet, enabling the crew to pull it from anywhere in the cockpit.

4. Pull the jib halyard until the head of the jib is close to the mast. The end of the rope halyard is attached to a wire loop which fits onto a hook on a multi-purchase downhaul. Pulling this downhaul will provide maximum tension on the jib luff (leading edge) which is vital for good sailing performance.

If the luff is not taut, the boat will not be able to point high upwind.

5. When the jib is rigged, its wire luff acts as the forestay which supports the mast, irrespective of whether the jib is furled or unfurled. The temporary rope forestay is used to hold the mast up while the boat is being rigged. Dan attaches it to the spinnaker bar, offset on one side to ensure it will not interfere with furling the jib. Alternatively, the temporary forestay can be attached to the mast where it is well out of the way.

6. Windward and leeward jib sheets are led through fairleads and jamming cleats on either side of the cockpit. Make sure they are correctly led by unrolling the jib and pulling both sheets in.

The Spinnaker

1. Use a bowline to attach the halyard to the head of the spinnaker and the spinnaker pole line to the tack. Unlike a loop, this will provide maximum security when the spinnaker is hoisted and dropped. The three corners of the sail should be clearly marked:

- HEAD (halyard)
- CLEW (sheet)
- TACK (pole)

2. The spinnaker halyard operates as a long continuous line. One end is attached to the head of the spinnaker which runs through the spinnaker chute and back into the cockpit, enabling the crew to pull it up or down. The other end is led through rings to a cross-patch in the centre of the spinnaker to pull it down into the chute. Use a bowline at both ends for best security as shown in the photo.

3. The tack (front corner) of the spinnaker is attached to a short tack line on the end of the spinnaker pole. A bowline is best as the spinnaker is hoisted by pulling the halyard, the spinnaker pole is automatically pulled forwards out of the bows.

Spinnaker Sheets

The spinnaker sheet should operate as a continuous line, so the crew can pull it from anywhere in the cockpit. The sheet must pass round the front of the forestay and outside the shrouds, before it is led through a ratchet block on each side of the cockpit.

Use a loop knot to attach the spinnaker sheet to the clew of the spinnaker. Make a small loop halfway along the sheet, push it through the cringle, then pull the long ends of the sheet through the loop until it is tight against the cringle. Or: Attach both ends of the spinnaker sheet to the clew of the spinnaker. The simplest method is to use two tight bowlines.

The two loose ends of the spinnaker sheet must be securely tied together so you can pull any part of the sheet during a gybe.

Trial hoist

It is easy to make a mistake and hoist the spinnaker upside-down or inside the shrouds. A trial hoist and drop will ensure everything is correct. Do not attempt to do this in a strong wind! Find a sheltered spot in the lee of a building where you can pull up the spinnaker without it flogging out of control. Make sure that all control lines are securely attached to the spinnaker:

1. Halyard to the head.

2. Spinnaker pole line to the tack.

3. Retrieval line (other end of halyard which is led through the spinnaker chute) to the middle of the spinnaker.

4. Port and starboard sheets to the clew.

Use the retrieval line to pull the spinnaker inside the chute. Use the halyard to pull the head of the spinnaker all the way up to the mast. Check that port and starboard spinnaker sheets are correctly routed outside forestay and shrouds.

Finally...

• Slide the rudder onto the pintles (stainless steel pegs) and ensure the rudder locks down so it cannot fall off in a capsize. Lock the rudder blade so it cannot fall down while you pull the boat to the water.

• Make sure there is no water inside the hull. Make extra sure that drain plugs and hatches are securely fastened and water cannot get in!

 Hoisting the spinnaker on the water is not a good time to discover that you've rigged it upside down or inside the shrouds!

LAUNCHING & LANDING

The problem with launching and landing is that you are often on public display. It's worth checking the launch area carefully before you go afloat, both to avoid damage to your boat and damage to your pride!

Sideshore Wind

The top choice for sailing away from the shore and coming back in, with an easily controlled beam reach in both directions.

Wind blowing at right angles across your launch area may cause problems on the slipway. If the wind is strong, or the slipway is narrow, you will have to launch with the mainsail lowered or risk the boat being blown over. If the slipway is wide, you may be able to pull the boat down (or up) the slipway with a series of diagonal tacks. For instance, pull the boat bows-first down the slipway from left to right, then stern-first across the slipway from right to left until you reach the water.

Onshore Wind

- With the wind blowing onshore, the boat can be pulled bows-first down the slipway with the mainsail hoisted. If the slipway is particularly steep or slippery, you may need extra hands at the shrouds or transom to guard against a runaway descent!

- The main problem in an onshore wind is sailing away from the beach. You will need to beat into the wind to leave the shore, but cannot point high or steer properly until the centreboard and rudder blade are fully down. Always choose the tack which provides the best angle to take you away from the shore.

Beware of waves breaking on the launch area in stronger winds. If the boat is not sailing at full power to windward, each wave that hits the boat will drive it back to the shore.

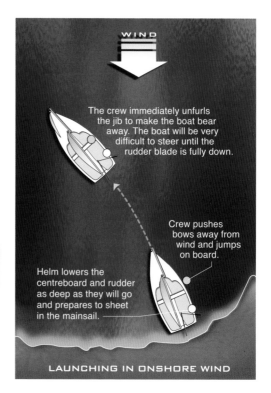

WIND

The crew immediately unfurls the jib to make the boat bear away. The boat will be very difficult to steer until the rudder blade is fully down.

Crew pushes bows away from wind and jumps on board.

Helm lowers the centreboard and rudder as deep as they will go and prepares to sheet in the mainsail.

LAUNCHING IN ONSHORE WIND

Offshore Wind

- With the wind blowing offshore, the boat can be pushed stern-first down the slipway with the mainsail hoisted. If the slipway is particularly steep or slippery again you may need extra hands to guard against a runaway descent!

- The main problem in an offshore wind is turning away from the shore. You need to allow enough space to turn the boat through an arc of more than 45°. To make the boat bear away from the wind and the shore, you need maximum power in the jib and minimum power in the mainsail. Heeling the boat to windward will help the boat bear away. The rudder will only be partially effective if the blade is not fully down.

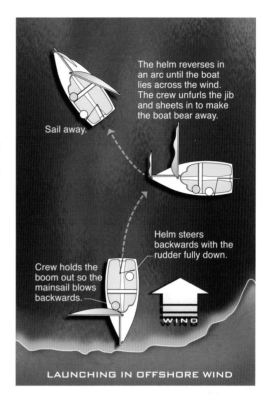

The helm reverses in an arc until the boat lies across the wind. The crew unfurls the jib and sheets in to make the boat bear away.

Sail away.

Helm steers backwards with the rudder fully down.

Crew holds the boom out so the mainsail blows backwards.

WIND

LAUNCHING IN OFFSHORE WIND

Steeply shelving beach at high water

Beware of deep water when you launch and land. If the water is deeper than your thighs, it may be difficult to hold the boat. Remember that the shore may change from gently shelving to steeply shelving between low and high tide.

Leaving the Trolley

Pull the boat into the water until it just starts to float, then push it back off the trolley. One crew needs to hold the boat by the bow while the other crew takes the trolley back up the slipway. Leave your trolley above the high water mark. Be thoughtful and do not obstruct the slipway or beach.

Check Tides

If you are in a tidal area, make sure you know the times of high and low tide and understand how the rise and fall will affect your launch area. For instance, you may launch on a concrete slipway at high tide and come ashore on sinking mud at low tide!

Sailing Away from the Shore

The crew can get into the cockpit to prepare the boat for sailing – pull down some Cunningham tension to put power in the mainsail, partly lower the centreboard and rudder blade, make sure the mainsheet runs free.

1. The helm pushes the bow away from the wind, which now blows at an angle of about 40° onto the port side of the bow. He lets the boat drift forward and holds on by the windward shroud.

2. As soon as the crew is ready, the helm pushes the boat forward and steps smartly into the back of the cockpit. On some dinghies, it is easier to step in through the open transom.

3. The crew uncleats the furling line and pulls in the leeward sheet as soon as the helm steps on board. This will help the dinghy to accelerate away from the beach.

4. Steering will be heavy and unresponsive with the rudder partly lifted – do not sheet in the mainsail and attempt to steer with the rudder until there is enough water to lock the blade in the fully-down position. Pulling in the leeward jib sheet will make the boat bear away and provide an alternative method of steering the boat.

1. Dan holds the boat by the windward shroud. Bryony climbs on board and partially lowers the centreboard and rudder as far as possible in the shallow water.

2. Dan moves back, grabs the tiller and steps into the back of the cockpit, pushing off with his foot.

3. Dan grabs the mainsheet. Bryony unfurls the jib to swing the bows away from the wind.

4. Steering with a half-raised rudder is heavy and unresponsive. As soon as it is deep enough, Dan lets go of the mainsheet to slow the boat, then locks the rudder fully down. Bryony lowers the centreboard to the fully down position, which will provide optimum performance sailing away from the land.

Landing in an Onshore Wind

Coming ashore with the wind behind can be tricky –
it may be difficult to stop the boat. If you have any
doubts, the best method is to drop the mainsail
before approaching the shore.

- Turn into the wind, let go the halyard and roll the
  mainsail in the cockpit.

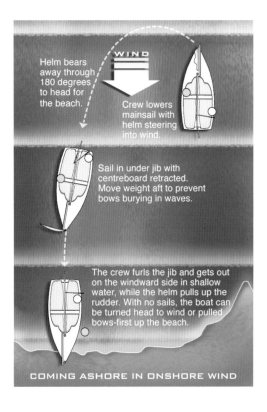

Helm bears away through 180 degrees to head for the beach.

Crew lowers mainsail with helm steering into wind.

Sail in under jib with centreboard retracted. Move weight aft to prevent bows burying in waves.

The crew furls the jib and gets out on the windward side in shallow water, while the helm pulls up the rudder. With no sails, the boat can be turned head to wind or pulled bows-first up the beach.

COMING ASHORE IN ONSHORE WIND

Landing in an Offshore Wind

- Make a slow and controlled approach under the
  jib, which can be furled as soon as it is shallow
  enough to jump out and hold the boat.

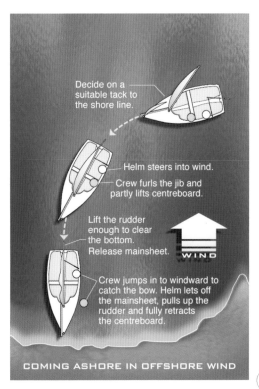

Decide on a suitable tack to the shore line.

Helm steers into wind.

Crew furls the jib and partly lifts centreboard.

Lift the rudder enough to clear the bottom. Release mainsheet.

Crew jumps in to windward to catch the bow. Helm lets off the mainsheet, pulls up the rudder and fully retracts the centreboard.

COMING ASHORE IN OFFSHORE WIND

Picking up a mooring

A recreational dinghy like the Vision has a heavy hull which takes time to stop! Always make a slow, cautious approach. It is easy to approach too fast and overshoot. If there is tide flowing, always make your final approach against the tide. Otherwise you will be swept past the mooring. Even if the crew manages to grab a hold, it may be impossible to hang on. Only use the mainsail if you can make the final approach upwind. In all other situations it will be easiest to drop the mainsail before your final approach. The jib will provide sufficient power until the crew lets the sheet fly as you come alongside. Aim to grab the buoy by the shrouds on the windward side. Have a painter attached to the bow which can be looped round the buoy and back to the dinghy. Lift the centreboard while the boat is lying on the mooring.

1. Dan approaches with the mainsail dropped. Bryony controls speed with the jib.

2. She lets the jib sheet go and grabs the pick-up buoy.

3. Use a painter to secure the boat to the mooring.

4. When leaving, Dan opts to reverse away with mainsail hoisted.

Coming Alongside

If you need to come alongside another boat, first advice is to choose a RIB with forgiving inflatable sides. Second advice is to always come alongside to leeward with your sails blowing away from the boat. This makes it easy to come alongside and get away, since you will naturally be blown away from the boat. If you come alongside to windward, you risk hitting people in the boat with the boom, being blown over on top of them and getting pinned to the boat when you want to depart. In some situations it may only be possible to come alongside to windward. Drop the mainsail before your final approach and roll up the jib as you come alongside.

 Always come alongside to leeward if possible. The safest possible approach is with mainsail dropped. Bryony has just rolled away the jib.

Reducing sail area

It is easier to reef the mainsail on dry land, but with skill you can do it on the water. Best practice is to 'heave-to' by pulling in the jib on the windward side and pushing the tiller in the opposite direction – the dinghy should drift slowly with the wind, without heading up or bearing away.

The crew eases off the main halyard and pulls down hard on the dual reefing line, until leech and luff cringles are pulled tight against the boom. She then tensions the main halyard and rolls the reefed sail neatly alongside the boom.

POINTS OF SAILING & MAXIMUM SPEED

The principal points of sailing – beating towards the wind, reaching across the wind and running with the wind – are determined by the angle of your course to the apparent wind. Trimming the boat and sails correctly will provide easy handling with maximum speed.

Beating Upwind Wind is blowing across the windward side of the bows.

- Crew weight is moved forward to lift the stern and depress the bows, which increases waterline length. Both crew need to hike off the side decks to hold the boat level.

- Mainsheet and jib sheet are sheeted hard in. The helm steers the boat at the optimum angle to the apparent wind with telltales streaming.

- Centreboard should be fully down, but may be partly lifted if it makes the boat easier to handle in stronger winds.

- If the boat heels more than a few degrees, the side of the hull will sink in the water and slow it down. The helm should ease the mainsheet to lose power and stay upright in gusts.

- The slot between jib and mainsail accelerates airflow over the leeward side of the mainsail. Letting out the jib sheet will open the slot and reduce power, which is a useful trick when you are hit by a strong gust of wind.

- Gnav or kicker (vang) tension is not required to hold the boom down. The outhaul has maximum tension to reduce camber (fullness) in the mainsail. The Cunningham is tensioned to flatten the mainsail and move the centre of effort (main pressure area) closer to the mast, depowering the sail as the wind increases.

- If waves are hitting the bows and slowing the boat, it will pay to bear off slightly and go for more speed. Move crew weight slightly aft to help lift the bows, particularly in stronger winds.

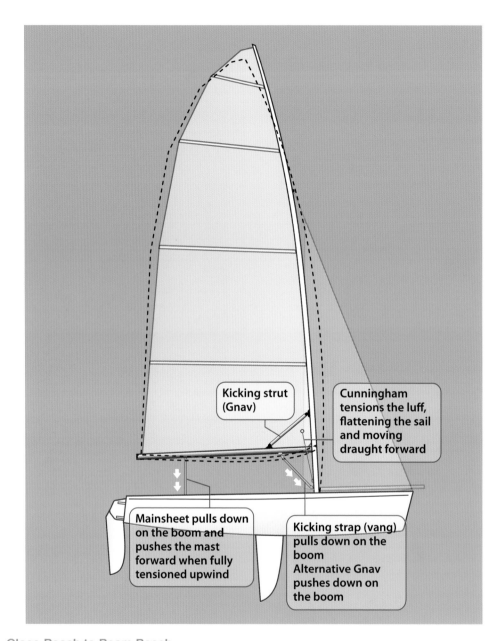

Kicking strut (Gnav)

Cunningham tensions the luff, flattening the sail and moving draught forward

Mainsheet pulls down on the boom and pushes the mast forward when fully tensioned upwind

Kicking strap (vang) pulls down on the boom
Alternative Gnav pushes down on the boom

Close Reach to Beam Reach

Wind is blowing across the boat.

- The boat is planing in a Force 3 breeze, indicated by a flat wake behind the stern. Crew weight is moved back to lift the bows. Both crew hike off the side decks to hold the boat level. If the boat stops planing due to a lull in the wind, both crew should slide forward to prevent the stern dragging.

- Mainsheet and jib sheet are trimmed to keep telltales streaming aft and hold the boat upright. The slot still plays a major role in accelerating airflow around the mainsail.

- Centreboard may be partly lifted to balance the boat. Trial and error will determine if this makes it easier to steer.

- Gnav tension holds the boom down. Both outhaul and Cunningham are tensioned to reduce camber and flatten the mainsail, with the centre of effort well forward for easier control.

Running Downwind Wind is blowing across the windward side of the stern.

- Crew weight is far enough forward to prevent the stern dragging and slowing the boat. Both crew sit inside the cockpit near the centreline to balance the boat.

- Centreboard may be partly or fully lifted to help balance the boat.

- The mainsheet is eased off until the boom almost touches the shroud. Gnav tension is required to hold the boom down. Cunningham and outhaul control lines can be eased to promote a fuller sail shape.

- The jib sheet is eased as far as possible without the sails collapsing. If the helm bears away and sail deeper downwind, the jib will be completely blanketed by the mainsail and provide no power.

Do not drag the stern

- The boat must be correctly trimmed fore and aft. Sailing upwind in light or moderate winds, it is normal to shift crew weight as far forward as the windward shroud. This helps lift the transom to prevent it dragging and slowing the boat down. It also pushes down the bows, which will increase waterline length for a slight boost in performance.

Move Along the decks

- As boat speed increases, the stern will lift and the bows will start to get pushed down. The crew must move their weight aft to let the bows skim the water, without burying and dragging the stern. Depending on the type of boat and conditions, constant fore and aft movement may be required to ensure optimum trim. Sailing 'by the seat of the pants' is the best way to assess how the boat is performing, but requires a backlog of experience.

Sail flat at all times

All modern dinghies are designed to be sailed as upright as possible. If you let a dinghy heel too far to leeward, it will:

1. Slip sideways, due to less resistance from the centreboard or daggerboard.

2. Lose power, due to less pressure driving the sails.

3. Slow down, due to the side of the hull burying in the water.

4. Be difficult to steer, due to a natural tendency to turn into the wind (weather helm). This will be even more difficult to control if the rudder blade is partly lifted out of the water.

The solution is to keep the dinghy flat by hiking out harder, easing the mainsheet or luffing into the wind during gusts. If the rig is permanently overpowered, the mainsail can be depowered by tensioning the Cunningham and kicking strap (vang). This will move the centre of effort forward and twist open the top of the sail, allowing airflow to escape without powering up the rig. On a double-handed boat, airflow between the mainsail and jib can be reduced by using a barber hauler to move the jib sheet further outboard, which will widen the slot between the sails. If necessary, partly lift the centreboard or daggerboard to reduce heeling moment.

Trimming the sheets

The mainsheet controls the horizontal angle of the mainsail, which is like a curved foil with wind flow divided over its windward and leeward surfaces. Pulling the mainsheet in tight when sailing upwind will also increase leech tension.

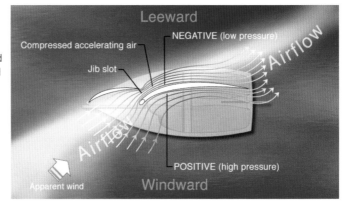

- Virtually all modern dinghies have a centre mainsheet, which the helm pulls through a block in the middle of the cockpit. Most dinghies are fitted with an auto-ratchet block, which can be set to 'on' (you can hear the clicks as it locks) or off (free running for faster response, but harder to hold). This enables the helm to respond immediately to a gust by letting out the mainsheet, which will depower the rig and prevent the boat heeling.

- The jib sheet is used to adjust the horizontal angle of the jib. Pulling the sheet in tight will increase both leech and foot tension. Some dinghies have an adjustable sheeting angle, providing greater tension on the foot or jib.

Jib telltales

Wind streams over both sides of a sail, creating high pressure on the windward side and low pressure on the leeward side, which pulls and sucks the sail.

- Telltales are lightweight streamers – sometimes known as 'woolies' – attached at different heights near the leading edge of a sail. Sailing upwind, the windward telltales should be starting to stream slightly upwards, with the leeward telltales streaming back horizontally.

- If windward side telltales stop streaming, you either need to pull in the sheet or bear away. If leeward side telltales stop streaming, you either need to ease out the sheet or head up.

- Windward telltales provide instant feedback when sailing upwind or on a reach; leeward telltales will be slower to respond to changes in wind flow.

- There are normally two or three sets of telltales at different heights. They will not all stream perfectly in unison. Owing to sail twist (the leech of the sail is more open at the top), upper telltales may start to lift while lower telltales still stream aft. However lower telltales are most important, since they provide feedback on the sail area with maximum power.

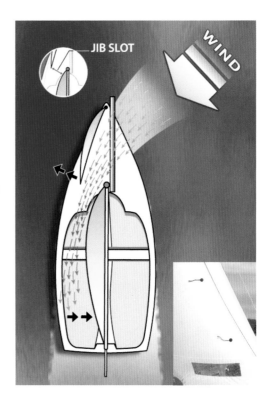

How high can you point when beating upwind?

In perfect conditions, with Force 3-4 on flat water – a dinghy like the Vision could be sailed at an angle of about 30° to the apparent wind. There is a fine line between pointing too high and slowing the boat, or pointing too low and sailing a longer distance. How high you can point will depend on the efficiency of the hull, foils and rig, your sailing ability and wind and sea state. It will never be possible to point at a constant angle to the wind, particularly in gusty conditions when your course may keep changing through 5-10°.

Watch the windward telltales to steer the boat as close to the wind as possible, ensuring there is clean airflow across the sails. Use intuition and feel to match your course to the wind. Watch gusts blowing across the water towards the windward side of the bows. Be ready to respond by hiking hard or easing the mainsheet.

The effect of Apparent Wind

True wind is wind direction and speed blowing onto a fixed object, such as a sailing club anemometer. Apparent wind is wind direction and speed blowing onto a moving object. It increases when sailing towards the wind and decreases when sailing away from the wind. The speed of the boat through the water alters the angle of the apparent wind. As the boat accelerates, apparent wind swings forward. Jib sheet and mainsheet must be pulled in tighter to keep the telltales flying for correct trim.

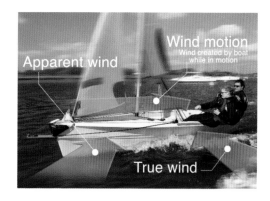

Try sailing with no rudder

Sail trim and boat trim are the two main ingredients required to sail a boat at the fastest possible speed. The best way to get a perfect understanding of trim is to practise without a rudder. Pull the rudder blade clear of the water for this exercise. You should be able to beat, reach, run, tack and gybe by moving body weight and trimming the sheets. The boat will be more responsive if you partly lift the centreboard. If the boat heels to leeward, it will turn into wind. Pulling in the mainsheet will also turn the boat into wind, due to loading up the centre of effort which is behind the centre of lateral resistance, provided by the centreboard. If the boat heels to windward, it will steer away from the wind. Letting out the mainsheet (depowering) and pulling in the jib (powering up) will have the same effect. Conversely, if the boat heels to leeward, it will be difficult to steer away from the wind. If the boat heels to windward, it will be difficult to steer towards the wind. The rudder helps steer the boat and provides fine-tuning, but must be used in conjunction with sail and boat trim for maximum effectiveness. The rudder will be least effective at high speeds, when sail and boat trim should dictate where the boat goes. Too much use of the rudder will act as a brake which slows the boat down.

Heel to windward with jib powered to bear away.

Heel to leeward with mainsail powered to head up.

Keep heeling and the boat will turn head to wind.

Let the mainsheet go and power up the jib to complete a rudderless tack.

TACKING A TWIN-CREW BOAT

Changing tacks is a vital skill when sailing upwind. Good technique is required to steer through the tack while controlling the tiller and mainsheet from different sides of the boat. Both crew play an important role in making the tack a fast and fluid turn.

What the helm must do...

1. Hold the tiller extension across the front of your body, using a dagger grip with the back hand.

2. Ease the mainsheet as you steer into the tack.

3. Stand up and pivot through 180°, facing forwards, as you cross the cockpit. Keep the mainsheet in your front hand and continue to steer the boat through the tack with your back hand.

4. Let your hand swivel around the tiller extension as you move to the new side. You will also need to angle the tiller extension, to ensure it can fit through the gap between cockpit, mainsheet and boom.

5. Move onto the new side, holding the tiller extension with the same hand, which is now crossed behind your back, while your other hand continues to hold the mainsheet.

6. Sheet in and get the boat settled on the new tack and sailing in the right direction. If it's heeling over, hike out to pull the boat flat.

7. When you're ready for the hand transfer, move the mainsheet hand onto the lower part of tiller extension. Then immediately flick the tiller extension across the front of your body and grab the sheet with your new front hand. If you are finding this difficult, a likely solution is to sit further forward on the side deck.

8. Pull in and trim the mainsheet for your new course.

1. Dan and Bryony get the boat sailing upwind at good speed.

2. Dan pushes the tiller right over as both crew move into the cockpit.

3. Bryony keeps the jib backed to help pull the bows round, while Dan eases the mainsheet.

4. Dan pivots onto the side with the tiller extension behind his back.

5. Dan changes hands on tiller extension and mainsheet as Bryony sheets in the jib and prepares to move onto the side.

6. They hike to pull the boat flat and power away on the new tack with mainsheet and jib sheeted in.

What the crew must do…

The crew provides important support, ensuring the jib helps pull the boat through the turn without stalling and transferring weight to help power away on the new tack.

1. As the helm steers into the tack, the crew keeps the jib sheeted in and moves into the middle of the boat.
2. The crew ducks under the boom while moving to the new side. The jib is left sheeted, so it back-winds and helps blow the bows round. This is important to help prevent the boat stalling head-to-wind.
3. As soon as the boat has successfully turned through the tack, the crew lets go the old sheet and pulls in hard on the new side. At the same time the crew moves smartly out onto the new side deck to balance the boat.

Communication

The helm tells the crew it's time to tack and waits for the crew to confirm they are ready.

Helm: "Ready to tack?"

Crew: "Ready!"

Helm: "Tacking!"

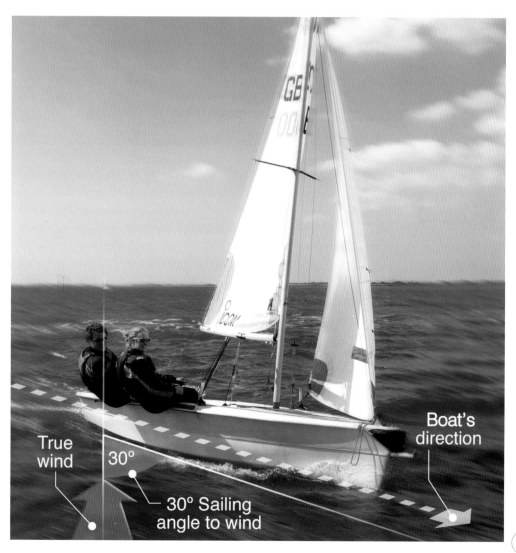

GYBING A TWIN-CREW BOAT

A gybe allows you to change tack while sailing downwind. Bearing away through the eye of the wind makes the boom swing across the cockpit to the new leeward side. This is a straightforward manoeuvre in light winds, which requires more skill as the wind increases, when a mistake will frequently cause a capsize.

What the helm must do...

1. Steer carefully through the turn – always be in full control of the rudder. Use continuous adjustment rather than one large rudder movement.
2. Keep the boat flat throughout the gybe – you may let the boat heel slightly to windward going into the gybe, to help it bear away. Sheeting in slightly helps power up the sail as the boat turns.
3. As soon as you are running by the lee (wind blowing over the new windward side of the stern), you can induce the mainsail to gybe by giving a sharp tug on the falls of the mainsheet. Some dinghies have a gybing strop attached to the boom for this purpose. If it won't gybe, you need to keep the boat turning. With experience it's possible to judge the right moment, as pressure goes light in the mainsail.
4. If you leave the boom to decide when it's time to gybe, it may wait until the boat has turned far enough for the wind to hit the back of the mainsail. That's ok in light winds, but in strong winds the boom will swing across and crash to the new side. The boat heels over, the helm loses control of steering and the boat keeps turning onto a beam reach leading to inevitable capsize.
5. As soon as the mainsail flicks across, straighten out the rudder on the new course, while the boat is still sailing deep downwind. Do not let the boat round up onto a reach, which will blow it onto its side.
6. The helmsman pivots round to the new windward side of the boat, using the same hand-to-hand technique as tacking. Sit well forward with the tiller extension held behind your back, grab the lower half of the tiller extension with your old sheet hand, flick the tiller extension across the front of your body, and grab the mainsheet with your new front hand to complete the gybe.

1. Dan looks for the spot to gybe.

2. He bears away at full speed and moves across the boat.

3. Dead downwind and ready for the gybe.

4. Dan flicks the boom across with a tug on the falls of the mainsheet.

5. Dan immediately straightens his course to keep sailing downwind, while Bryony sheets in on the new side.

6. Then tiller extension moved to the back hand and up on the new course with everything under control.

What the crew must do…

1. The crew moves into the cockpit during the gybe, but may need to move weight quickly to flatten the boat if the helm has less than perfect control.

2. Let off the jib sheet and pull in on the new side as the boom swings across the cockpit, if necessary changing from goosewing to goosewing on the windward side.

Keep your gybes tight

Gybing through the smallest possible angle is the best way to control the gybe in stronger winds. You only need to turn the boat through an arc that's big enough to gybe the mainsail. From there you can get the boat under control and choose where you want to sail – either keep running downwind or head up onto a reach. A wider gybe angle will require a greater course correction.

Keep your speed

The faster you sail through the gybe, the lighter the apparent wind will be on the rig, which should make it easier to control the sail. If the boat slows down, apparent wind will increase and make it more difficult to gybe the mainsail without upsetting the boat. This problem normally occurs because the helm gets frightened by the boat's speed and fails to steer a smooth curve into the gybe. The solution is to abort the gybe, luff back onto your original course, settle down and then try the gybe again.

Communication

The helm tells the crew it's time to gybe and waits for the crew to confirm they are ready.

Helm: "Ready to gybe?"

Crew: "Ready!"

Helm: "Gybing!"

USING A TRAPEZE

A trapeze is an optional extra on a dinghy like the Vision and provides the crew with more leverage to hold down the boat and a lot more fun! Learning to hang from a trapeze is highly recommended once you have mastered the basics of dinghy sailing!

How a trapeze works

A trapeze wire simply lets you stand on the side of the boat. This not only provides more leverage than hiking, but is also far more comfortable! Two trapeze wires are attached to the mast at the same height as the shrouds. The lower end of each trapeze wire has a plastic handle and a stainless steel ring, which may have an adjustable height feature. When not in use, the trapeze wire is kept taut by an elastic attached to the side deck.

Trapeze harness & hook

- A trapeze harness is fitted with a stainless steel hook which fits into the stainless steel ring on the end of the trapeze wire. To avoid danger of entrapment during a capsize – for instance being caught on a shroud – all modern hooks have a quick-release system.

- The harness is designed to spread the effort of trapezing across your hips and back, with adjustable straps for shoulders and legs and the hook pulled in tight. A comfortable fit is vital if you wish to trapeze for more than a few minutes at a time. Most people wear a harness under their buoyancy aid, but vice-versa works ok.

Getting on the wire

Sit on the side, with your front hand grab the plastic handle above the trapeze ring and hook on with your back hand.

Take your weight onto the trapeze wire and taking the jib sheet with you slide back. If the wire is too slack, adjust the ring to a higher position.

Step out of the boat with your front leg and then follow with your back leg, stand back with the support of the trapeze wire before letting go of the handle.

Relax with your weight on the wire with the balls of your feet on the side of the boat. Use your front leg as a brace and your back leg slightly bent and relaxed.

Holding the jib (or spinnaker sheet) will help maintain your balance.
If you start swinging forwards, a good trick is to grab the helm's buoyancy aid and use it as an anchor. If your helm is grumpy I suggest you warn them first!

Where do you stand?

Normal trapezing position when beating upwind is just aft of the shroud.

- Step back along the side deck when the boat sails on a reach

- Keeping your front leg braced against forward pull from the trapeze wire

- If waves keep hitting your body, move the trapeze ring to a higher position.

Standing on the side

The trapeze wire will tend to pull you forwards, particularly if you move back when sailing on a reach. Use the front leg to support most of your weight and the back leg to provide balance. Always try to stand with your feet close together when trapezing upwind. It not only looks neater but is also more efficient than a wide leg stance.

How high should you trapeze?

When you first learn trapezing, it's much easier with a high hook position, which is also required to stand further back on a reach or to lift your body above waves. For maximum leverage, flat out and virtually parallel to the water is most efficient but requires a greater physical challenge.

Getting in and out

- Bend your legs to weight in towards the boat in a lull.

- Straighten your legs to move your weight away from the boat in a gust.

Don't be a drag! Beware of falling in to windward if the wind drops. Always be ready to come in off the wire if power in the rig won't carry your weight.

Getting off the wire

1. Bend your front leg, while holding the jib (or spinnaker) sheet in your back hand, which provides support as you swing into the boat.

2. Move your back foot off the side deck and into the cockpit, supporting your body with your back hand.

3. Follow immediately with your front foot, so you are crouching in a semi-hiking position.

4. Push the trapeze ring off the hook with your back hand; let go of the handle with your front hand.

SPINNAKER SAILING

An asymmetric spinnaker provides turbo-charged power for broad reaching downwind. It not only provides a lot of extra fun for modern dinghy sailors, but is also a surprisingly easy sail to control.

Full speed downwind

Asymmetric spinnakers are designed for reaching at maximum speed. Gybing from broad reach to broad reach can provide optimum VMG – velocity made good – when sailing downwind. Unlike a classic symmetrical spinnaker, an asymmetric is not designed for running directly downwind when it is blanketed by the mainsail. An asymmetric also requires far more space on the water, which can make it unsuitable for sailing on small reservoirs and lakes.

Spinnaker, jib and mainsail are sheeted in parallel, providing a double slot effect to accelerate wind between the sails.

Asymmetric controls

An asymmetric spinnaker has one clew attached to a continuous sheet, which allows the crew to trim from either side. The tack is attached to a pole, which is normally pulled out from the bows when the spinnaker is hoisted and retracted when the spinnaker is dropped. The halyard and retrieval line is a continuous line led back to the cockpit, enabling the crew to pull the spinnaker up the mast or back down into its chute.

Basic technique

Asymmetric technique is straightforward. Head up towards the wind to heat up power in the spinnaker, then bear away when the boat starts to heel to stay flat and sail as deep as possible downwind. The harder the wind blows, the deeper you can sail. The helm controls the balance of the boat, by bearing away to prevent the boat heeling to leeward when the spinnaker is overpowered, and then heading up to prevent the boat heeling to windward when the spinnaker is underpowered.

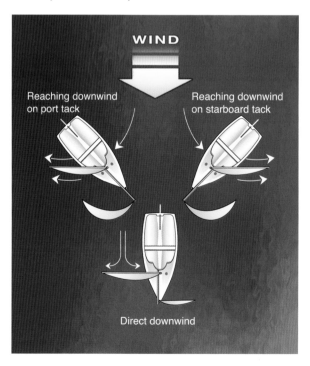

WIND

Reaching downwind on port tack

Reaching downwind on starboard tack

Direct downwind

The helm's role when hoisting the spinnaker...

Unless the wind is light, the helmsman must bear away deep downwind to ensure the spinnaker is blanketed by the mainsail during the hoist. If you attempt to hoist on a beam reach, the partly hoisted spinnaker may fill with wind and blow the boat over.

Dan concentrates on steering deep downwind, so the spinnaker will be blanketed by the mainsail during the launch. Bryony stands to pull in the halyard hand-over-hand, getting the spinnaker up as quickly as possible. Make sure the spinnaker is right up to the mast when you lock off the halyard.

The crew's role when hoisting the spinnaker...

The crew needs a wide leg stance to pull out maximum lengths of halyard arm over arm, with the aim of getting the spinnaker up as quickly as possible. Make sure the spinnaker is fully hoisted. If the head of the sail is not pulled all the way to block on the mast, the spinnaker will be more difficult to control. One way to be sure is to mark the halyard where it passes through the cleat in the fully up position. You can fix this with a dry land hoist. As soon as the spinnaker is hoisted, the crew pulls in the sheet and moves onto the side of the boat. Occasionally, the spinnaker may be twisted in a hourglass shape. A sharp pull on the sheet will normally pull the spinnaker straight. If that fails, a spinnaker gybe should do the trick.

If the spinnaker goes up with a twist, you can try pulling the sheet. If that doesn't work, gybe immediately and sheet in on the new side.

The twist will disappear like magic!

Perfect trim! The boat is held bolt upright, leaving a flat wake at the stern.

Sailing with a spinnaker

Sailing at full power downwind requires the optimum course. Not too low to go slow; not too high to be overpowered. Your course should look like a wiggling snake. Head up towards the wind to increase power in the spinnaker, then bear away and accelerate on the apparent wind for optimum VMG. The boat will only respond to steering with an asymmetric when it is sailed flat. If the boat heels to leeward, bear away immediately to keep the rig upright while chasing the apparent wind. If the boat starts to slow down and heels to windward, head up to increase sail power.

The helm steers the right course...

The helm has to steer the boat to keep it flat on the water, following the spinnaker as it drives the dinghy downwind at maximum speed. The view to leeward may be obscured by the spinnaker, but the helm must keep a lookout and be prepared to give way to other boats. Port always gives way to starboard. A boat sailing downwind must give way to a boat sailing upwind on the same tack.

The crew trims the spinnaker...

The crew concentrates on trimming the spinnaker.

- Hold the sheet with both hands and watch the top half of the luff

- Ease the sheet until the luff is just starting to curl

- If there is no curl, the sail is over sheeted and will not provide full power – ease the sheet out.
  If there is too much curl, the sail will collapse – pull the sheet in

- Try to keep a slight curl on the luff for maximum performance.

Bryony sheets the spinnaker so the leading edge is just starting to fold inwards, indicating full power in the sail without stalling wind flow. If the leading edge starts to collapse, it's time to sheet in or bear away. Meanwhile, Dan is about to 'reverse' the tiller extension prior to a gybe.

Way too much heel! The boat will slow right down and start careering up towards the wind. When a gust hits, always hold the boat flat and bear away.

The helm's role when gybing...

The helmsman should keep the boat as flat as possible throughout the gybe, while concentrating on steering with the boat moving fast to minimise apparent wind. If you slow down to 10 knots when gybing in 20 knots true wind, apparent wind will build to 10 knots. If you let the boat slow to 5 knots, apparent wind will build to 15 knots and make control more difficult as the main boom swings to the new side.

1. Sailing at full speed, Dan bears away downwind.

2. Dan tugs the falls of the mainsheet to gybe the mainsail as the stern turns through dead downwind.

3. Bryony keeps tension on the old sheet until she pulls the new sheet in. This prevents the spinnaker blowing forward and wrapping round itself.

4. Fully powered up on the new course.

Gybing with a spinnaker

The sheet is the only control line that needs to be operated when gybing an asymmetric spinnaker. This simplicity allows a rapid transition from fully powered on one gybe to fully powered on the other gybe, with little loss of speed. By contrast gybing a conventional spinnaker is a complex procedure!

The crew's role when gybing...

To maintain power and speed, the crew should keep the spinnaker sheet pulled in as he comes in off the side deck. Start pulling the new sheet in hand-over-hand, from the middle of the cockpit, while moving out to the new windward side. The spinnaker can be over sheeted when the crew starts hiking, before letting a small amount of sheet to run out and get the luff curling when the helm luffs to windward and heats up the power.

The helm's role when dropping the spinnaker...

Bear away downwind to take pressure out of the spinnaker. This will allow the crew to move into the middle of the cockpit and grab the retrieval line, with the mainsail blanketing the spinnaker for the drop.

1. Bryony takes in slack on the retrieval line, before uncleating the halyard. This ensures that the spinnaker is pulled back and will not drop over the bows.

2. Dan steers deep downwind to depower and blanket the spinnaker during the drop. Bryony pulls the retrieval line hand-over-hand.

3. Stand up to pull if the spinnaker appears to jam in chute. Make sure you are not standing on the halyard and that the cleat is off.

4. The spinnaker pole retracts automatically as the spinnaker is pulled inside the chute.

The crew's role when dropping the spinnaker...

• As you come in off the side deck, place a foot on the spinnaker sheet. This will keep the spinnaker filling while you pull in any slack on the retrieval line. Taking slack out of the retrieval line pulls the spinnaker back towards the mast and helps ensure it will pull neatly into the chute. If you fail to do this, half the spinnaker may drop down over the bows and into the water.

• Uncleat the halyard and pull the retrieval line in hand-over-hand as quickly as possible. If the line jams, there are three likely problems. First, you are standing on the halyard. Second, the halyard cleat has inadvertently snapped shut on the line. Third, the line is jammed by a tangle of spaghetti. If there is still a problem, pull the spinnaker back up and then drop it again.

• You do not need to strain any muscles to get the spinnaker back into the chute. If it is stuck, pulling hard may rip the material. Best solution is to pull the spinnaker back up, take all tension out of the retrieval line, then pull it back down again.

CAPSIZE

The skipper (normally the helm) has responsibility for the safety and enjoyment of the crew. Ensuring that any capsizes are safe and controlled is a fundamental requirement on board a twin-crew boat. It is a good idea to have a pre-arranged plan as to what everyone should do in the event of a capsize. This saves all the repercussions afterwards!

Going over

The standard capsize to leeward takes place when a dinghy is blown over by too much power in the sails. The simple solution is to let go the sheets to depower the sails and hike like mad, but sometimes it's just too late!

1. Point of no return. Let all sheets fly.

2. Leg over! It's the helm's prerogative to hop over the side and stay dry.

3. If the spinnaker is hoisted, it must be pulled back inside the chute.

4. The Vision has righting lines under the gunwale, which makes it easy for Dan to lean back.

5. When the mast lifts from the water, holding it just above the surface will help the rig to blow downwind.

6. Dan leans back to complete the retrieval. Bryony is scooped into the cockpit while Dan hops in from the windward side.

Who gets wet?

It is the helm's prerogative to stay dry! He simply vaults onto the centreboard and leaves the crew to fall in the water. (This technique works just as well on a single-handed boat, with no argument about who gets wet!)

Down in the water

Bryony falls in the water between the boom and cockpit. It is important to resist the temptation to hang on to the upper deck, which will pull the capsized dinghy into full inversion. For the same reason, it's best not to stand on the boom or mast.

- Bryony makes sure that the mainsheet and jib sheets will run free, so there's no power in the sails when the boat is pulled upright. If it's windy, she may also let off the Cunningham and reduce leech tension, further depowering the mainsail.

Pulling the boat upright

- Dan leans back against the righting line to lift the rig. If the boat has blown downwind of the rig, lift the mast just clear of the water and wait for the bows to pivot round into the wind. Then lean back and continue lifting the rig.

- The boat will come upright more and more quickly as the rig lifts higher. The helm scrambles over the windward side while the crew scrambles over the leeward side, or is already on the leeward deck, with both crew balancing the boat.

Sail with a knife
A small number of fatal accidents have been caused by the crew or helm getting trapped under the boat. Communication is key. A useful precaution is for both crew to always carry a security knife in the front pockets of their buoyancy aids. In an emergency, being able to cut elastic or rope could save a life.

Upside down?

Most modern dinghies are designed to shed water from the cockpit. This is achieved by having a shallow cockpit with a thick double bottom which slopes from the bows to the open transom where all water immediately drains. This is great, but has one major downside. Dinghies with high volume in the bottom of the hull can easily invert. This normally happens if the crew hangs on and pulls the boat upside-down, if the mast fills with water and sinks due to being poorly sealed, or when the boat capsizes with a lot of momentum and the helm cannot jump on the centreboard – often as the result of an out-of-control gybe.

If the boat inverts, both crew must immediately check their partner is OK. The last stage of the inversion should be gradual and provide plenty of time to get clear of the hull. In the unlikely event that you are underneath an upturned boat, don't panic. Duck out from the side or transom, which may require a hard push due to your buoyancy aid constricting movement through the water.

1. Dan gives Bryony a hand up, standing on the underside of the gunwale.

2. Dan and Bryony lean back to float the rig. If it won't come up, the mast is probably stuck in the mud!

3. Dan hops onto the centreboard as the rig floats to the surface.

4. Bryony swims round the transom to continue the retrieval.

Bringing it back up

The Vision provides a stable platform floating upside-down. Dan climbs up on the hull and grabs the righting line. He ensures the centreboard is fully down, before helping Bryony to join him on the hull.

• Standing on the upturned gunwale, Dan and Bryony lean back against the centreboard and righting line. This will slowly float the rig to the surface, until Dan can climb onto the centreboard and hold the boat on its side.

• Bryony drops back into the water and swims round the transom to the cockpit. She ensures all sheets are running free before Dan pulls the boat upright and scoops her into the cockpit.

High performance sailing requires an easily driven hull, a powerful rig and a good breeze. The pleasures of sailing any high performance dinghy include crisp, immediate response, with good technique required to keep control at speed in stronger winds. The RS500 ticks all the boxes, with glassfibre foam sandwich for light weight, stiffness and durability, Mylar® sails for light weight and minimum stretch, plus a 14 square metre spinnaker to provide rocketship sailing downwind.

Helm: James Peters – World Sailing Youth World
Champion in 29er

Crew: Stevie Wilson – 29er European Champion

Conditions: Force 3-5

97

BEFORE LEAVING THE BEACH

James and Stevie demonstrate that rigging needs to be methodical and fault-free, ensuring there will be no unexpected problems on the water…

Stevie lifts the mast onto the deck of the RS500, while James appears to take an unnatural interest in seagulls, before attaching upper and lower shrouds.

Stevie makes sure the trapeze wires are securely attached to the mast. He relies on them!

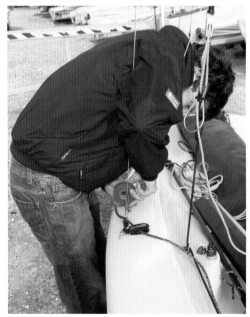

James wraps the shroud plates with electric tape. This will ensure the pins cannot fall out and protect vulnerable spinnaker cloth from sharp edges. More tape protection is required below the tack of the jib.

Upper shrouds hold the mast up. Lower shrouds help to control mast bend induced by the boom. The chainplates have different holes to adjust mast rake.

It pays to be tidy, especially on a day with big waves and fresh wind. James coils the end of the halyard neatly before stowing it away.

James uses both hands to pull up the halyard while Stevie guides the boltrope.

Going up! Stevie prepares to feed the boltrope into the mast slot while James hoists the main halyard hand-over-hand.

Check List

- Make sure there is no water inside the hull and inspection hatches are locked tight.

- Tape over any sharp edges that may snag the spinnaker. Tape over pins in shroud plates to ensure they cannot fall out.

- Check control lines and elastics for wear.

- Set up the correct rig tension and mast rake for prevailing wind and sea conditions before you leave the beach.

- Coil and stow loose ends of the mainsail and jib halyard, ensuring they will run free if you need to drop sails quickly when landing.

- Test trapeze wires for security and set the height of the rings.

SAILING UPWIND

Sailing a high performance boat upwind is all about VMG (velocity made good). Do not try to point as high as possible towards the wind. Crack off a few degrees and go for speed…

Always sail flat

The boat is bolt upright, with lots of kicker (vang) and Cunningham tension to depower the mainsail. James is flat hiking rather than drop hiking to keep his bottom out of the water, which puts more load on stomach muscles than quads. Stevie is wiring as low as possible, but high enough not to hit oncoming waves or make James have to heel the boat to lift him clear.

Keep close

Crew weight should be very close together upwind, but always leave a small gap for the crew to step back and avoid ploughing a wave, which will take on water and slow the boat. Apart from tacks, the crew should always hand-hold the jib sheet, trimming through gusts and lulls in conjunction with the mainsheet.

Maximum power

Stevie's arm is on the way out behind his head, increasing leverage to hold more mainsheet = more power = more forward speed. James is tilting his head back to provide a small extra dose of leverage, an unconventional tweak that he's adopted over the years!

TROUBLE-FREE TACKING

Entry to the tack

James and Stevie look ahead to spot boats crossing on starboard tack. Setting up for a clean, fast tack is a critical manoeuvre. Encouraging a small dose of leeward heel helps the boat carve round into the tack.

Coming off the wire

Stevie bends his legs to come into the boat as James pushes the tiller slightly away, with enough drive to start the boat spinning through the tack.

Turning through the tack

Stevie stays on the windward side and rolls the boat with James, keeping the jib cleated before picking up the sheet on the new side.

Crossing to the new side

James and Stevie cross at the same time. James uses a 'gunwale grab' to stabilise the middle of the roll tack, while Stevie hits the handle to get weight out as fast as possible.

Steering into the new tack

James will not swap hands until the boat is flat on the new tack. This enables him to concentrate on steering and mainsheet trim all the way through to turn. Stevie adopts a dynamic position hanging from the handle with one hand whilst cleating the jib.

Driving out of the tack

Stevie is out on trapeze handle after a tack to get weight out as fast as possible – he always does this on his front hand. The jib is cleated before he goes to clip on with his other hand. James is heeling the boat over slightly to avoid dunking Stevie in the enormous oncoming wave, although 'boat flat and driving out of the tack' would normally be first priority.

SAILING DOWNWIND

Launching the spinnaker doubles sail area and provides a thrilling ride as you gybe downwind, going high and low to heat the boat up on apparent wind…

Spinnaker set-up

Use a bowline to securely attach the halyard to the head. The bowline must be pulled tight to the cringle, to ensure the head is pulled right up to the block on the mast.

Finding the corners.

Attaching the halyard.

Using a bowline attach the other end of the halyard to the patch in the middle of the spinnaker. The halyard/retrieval line is a continuous loop from the head of the spinnaker to a block on the mast, down through the mast to a fairlead at deck level in the cockpit, backwards through a jamming cleat to lock the halyard, through a return block and forwards through the chute, emerging from the mouth of the chute with the end attached to the patch in the middle of the spinnaker. A trial hoist ensures everything is correctly routed before you get on the water. It is a worthwhile precaution to ensure the spinnaker will slide in and out of its chute, with sheets passing outside the shrouds and forestay.

Attaching the retrieval line.

Pulling the spinnaker back through the chute.

Attaching spinnaker sheets

When attaching spinnaker sheets to the clew, one small knot is less likely to snag on the forestay than two big knots. An easy solution is to double the spinnaker sheet, push the eye of the loop through the cringle, then pull the two ends through to securely close the knot. To ensure the crew has a continuous lead, both loose ends should be tied together. Two opposing slip knots ensure the gennaker sheets are securely linked in the cockpit. The size and weight of the knot makes it easy for the crew to differentiate port and starboard sides of the sheet.

Spinnaker sailing at speed

Stevie's feet are right next to James, keeping their weight close together. The boat is being sailed as flat as possible with less kicker (vang) tension than upwind, but not fully released in strong winds. James holds the tiller in front of his body so he can play the mainsheet more efficiently with two hands, focused on holding the boat flat. Stevie looks relaxed, but watches the luff of the spinnaker like a hawk, tweaking the sheet every time it starts to fold.

Stevie looks totally relaxed on the wire – feet together, front leg straight, back leg bent, facing forward to trim the spinnaker as the luff curls. James sits in, keeping the boat flat at full speed.

PERFECT GYBES

Don't slow down, keep the boat flat and steer through a tight arc for a trouble-free high performance gybe, changing course through a maximum 20°…

1. James reverses the tiller while Stevie comes in, keeping tension on the spinnaker sheet.

2. James steers into the gybe with slight heel to windward. Stevie still has tension on the old sheet.

3. James steps across in one and corrects his steering as the boom gybes. Stevie still has tension on the old sheet.

4. James sits on the new deck before changing hands on tiller and mainsheet. Stevie moves out, extending his arm to pull in the sheet.

5. James bears away and prepares to lean forward and tweak the jibsheet. Stevie goes out on the trapeze handle, powering up the spinnaker before hooking in.

Good communication and practice between helm and crew is essential for stress-free gybes. Pick a clear area to sail downwind for 1.6km (1 mile), then keep gybing every 3 minutes, giving enough time for the boat to settle down before going straight into the next gybe. Take a rest when you can and do 10 perfect gybes in succession!

Entry to the gybe - Stage 1

- The boat is held flat or heeled slightly to windward, with the tiller pre-gybed to ensure there are no foul-ups. This is one of the most important things to get right when you gybe!

- James also pre-gybes the jib to enable Stevie to concentrate solely on gybing the kite. They time the gybe for when they are at maximum speed surfing a wave.

Pre-gybing the tiller

- During the entry, James has pre-gybed the tiller by flipping the extension to the new side. This means he can concentrate on steering through the gybe, with no worries about getting tangled in the mainsheet, also keeping the tiller well clear of Stevie who has come off the wire in conjunction with the helm's rate of turn.

- Note that Stevie is keeping as much of the old kite sheet pulled in as possible, instead of the natural tendency to let the sheet out as you move into the boat. This will prevent the clew from blowing round the luff in the entry to the gybe, which could lead to a spinnaker twist or slow exit with the kite not full.

Middle of the gybe - Stage 2

James takes one big step across the boat – shuffling is no way to go!

- He only swaps hands after sitting down on the new side.

- The helm needs to be aware of the crew's progress and adjust the speed of gybe accordingly.

- You can sail directly downwind for as long as necessary with the boom on the new gybe, which is the fully depowered angle with no need for the crew's weight to hold the boat level.

Exit from the gybe - Stage 3

A less than perfect exit because the spinnaker has a twist! This is due to too much kite sheet being let go on the entry, allowing the clew to get round the luff of the kite.

- Stevie has to pull the clew all the way to the block to get the twist out, whilst he is hanging on the trapeze handle. This is very slow as the kite is over trimmed for a few vital seconds.

- Stevie recovers the kite and eases the sheet to increase speed. The effects are obvious with the boat heeling slightly to windward. James should have prevented this by heading up, even though the boat felt powered up when the boom came across.

- Another gybe completed – the helm can lean forward to trim the jib!

1.

2.

1.

2.

Getting it wrong

So what's the problem with this gybe? The entry looks sweet, but things start to go wrong when James steers too fast through the turn. In the middle stage, he does not manage to make that big step to the other side, with too much weight on the old side making the boat heel over uncontrollably on the exit.

The best way to recover the situation is to keep the boat heading as far downwind as possible to keep the rig depowered.

1. You can see James attempting to steer downwind, but the rudder is spinning out due to the large amount of leeward heel.

2. Both crew need weight on the windward side so the mainsheet can be let off as much as possible.

3. The daggerboard also played an important role in this dodgy gybe. It wouldn't stay fully down which messed up the balance of the boat.

SAILING IN WAVES

Waves provide a recurring obstacle, making the boat more difficult to sail at speed and maintain control…

Upwind across waves

- If the waves are big rollers with wide troughs, it's like sailing through valleys and hills. Every time the boat is lifted by a wave, it is exposed to clean, strong wind; every time the boat sinks into a trough, the sails are partly blanketed by surrounding waves. Be prepared to ease the mainsheet and luff on wave tops, holding the boat flat by going full-out on the trapeze. Then bear away to maintain maximum power in the troughs, with the crew moving weight in as required.

- If the waves are steep and closely spaced – often the result of wind blowing against tide – the only way is to break through each face. This relies on speed and power. Bear off a few degrees to ensure the boat keeps powering ahead, instead of stalling when the bows hit each wave. If you are sailing through waves on a diagonal course, you may need to luff to hit each wave bows-on and prevent the hull being driven backwards.

- For maximum performance, set the mainsail up with enough power to sail through the troughs – not only camber in the foot, but also power in the head which will be exposed to the best of the wind. The mainsail will inevitably be overpowered on the tops, where the only solution is to ease the sheet until the boat drops into the next trough.

- Trim the boat aft to prevent the bow burying while sailing through waves. If necessary, move weight forward to sail up the backs and weight back to sail down the faces. The waves will of course provide a rocky ride. The helm needs to be well locked between the footstraps and side deck. Out on the trapeze, the crew needs to brace with the front leg against the forward pull of the wire, facing forward to watch the waves with feet spread to increase stability.

 As always, good communication between helm and crew will save the day!

Downwind on waves

- Be prepared for a high speed ride, sailing downwind on waves. The boat will accelerate like fury as it drops down wave faces, so bear away to keep the boat level with the apparent wind. Then luff to hold your speed, when sailing up the back of the next wave.

- Keep the bow flying with weight well back. It will be a disaster if the bow goes down the mine. Sailing at full bore on the face of a wave, the helm is right back at the transom with the crew alongside. In this position, there will be a lot of forward pull on the trapeze wire and spinnaker sheet. The crew needs a wide leg stance, with back leg heavily bent for 'suspension' and front leg providing an almost straight brace.

- Mainsheet and jib are trimmed for a close reach, with the kicker (vang) or gnav holding down the boom and maintaining sail twist. The taut mainsheet also plays an important role as a 'back stay' for the spinnaker. The crew trims the spinnaker on the apparent wind, watching the top third of the leech like a hawk, ready to tweak the sheet in as the leech starts to curl then the boat accelerates on apparent wind.

Sailing over waves on port tack

Waves don't come from the same angle as the wind, due to the spin of the earth. In this sequence they are almost side-on to the boat on port tack and would be bows-on sailing on starboard tack (fig. 1).

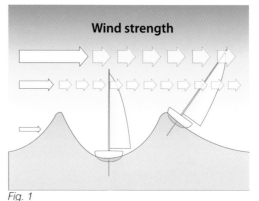

Wind strength

- Therefore Stevie needs to be higher (1) on the wire to prevent being hit by waves on port tack, but can trapeze lower for extra leverage on starboard.

- James and Stevie can also keep their bodyweight further forward on port tack (2), because waves are unlikely to swamp the boat when coming from the side.

Fig. 1

- The boat may be able to hold more kicker (vang) and point higher on port tack, thanks to the angle of the waves.

- As the wave approaches, James oversheets the mainsail enough to provide 5-10° of leeward heel and prevent Stevie hitting the wave.

- The lower Stevie is on the wire, the more heel will be required to stop him hitting the wave, with increased wind strength at the top of the wave also helping the boat to heel.

- Immediately after the wave has passed, James (3) ensures the boat is sailing flat.

1.

2.

3.

Catching a wave on starboard gybe

The waves are not coming from the same angle as the wind, so the RS500 is sailing diagonally across these waves on starboard gybe. This makes them harder to catch, but potentially more beneficial as the boat needs to be moving at a faster speed to stay on the wave at the same angle.

- The crew's actions are highly important as he is more mobile than the helm. It is therefore Stevie's job to make the boat catch each wave, which might be a flick or push in stronger winds and a 'move forward' in lighter winds.

- The helm is using the rudder to balance the boat. If it heels to leeward, James will bear away. If it heels to windward, James will head up.

- The mainsheet will probably be fairly static, but in lighter winds James might use it to pump and increase the chance of catching a wave. However, the crew's actions will have the major affect on successful wave-riding.

- The waves have a large effect on boat balance. There is loads of wind when the boat is on the top of a wave and surfing, simply because the rig is higher up in the air, allowing James to bear away and depower the boat down the wave.

- But as soon as they come off the back of the wave, the boat will be underpowered (2) where Stevie has to come off the wire to prevent heeling to windward. The ideal solution is for the helm to head up, get more power and keep the crew out on the wire.

1.

2.

3.

4.

Going down

Stevie gives a sharp jerk on his front foot to help the boat down the wave, making all the difference between catching and not catching a high speed ride. James leans forward to trim the jib (following a gybe), while bearing away to keep the boat flat with increased sail pressure on the top of the wave. Boat balance is in the rudder rather than the mainsheet, sailing at full speed downhill (4).

Reducing wetted area

The RS500 looks heavy on its stern, but James and Stevie are sailing in conditions that allow them to keep planing, which is more likely to reduce wetted area than drag the transom. Moving forward is likely to be a better technique for catching waves in lighter winds, when it may be beneficial for Stevie to shuffle forward on his toes in order to push the boat down the wave. But in stronger winds and on very big waves – as shown here – it will be more beneficial for the crew to 'flick' the boat down the wave by giving a short and sharp push on their front foot instead of actually moving forward in the boat.

Shop online at
www.rya.org.uk/shop

The RS200 is Britain's most popular twin-crew racing class. It combines powerful performance with superb responsiveness, which makes it a challenging boat to sail well. Every movement of the crew has a direct effect on handling and boat speed.

Helm: Frances Peters – World Sailing Youth World
Champion in 29er

Crew: Tom Walker – 29er, RS600, Formula 18

Conditions: Force 2-3

SHAPING THE MAINSAIL

Kicker (vang), outhaul and Cunningham tension are used to adjust the shape of the mainsail from full to flat, moving the power forward and bleeding excess power from the top of the leech as the wind increases…

Kicker (vang) tension

Kicker has been pulled on and the leech becomes tighter and more hooked. You need to control leech tension with the mainsheet in light winds, as kicker tension will bend the mast and depower the mainsail. When you need to ease the mainsheet in more wind, start to pull on kicker to maintain leech tension. Continue to pull on kicker on to depower the mainsail as it gets windier. But when it is super windy, easing off the kicker may increase control by enabling you to spill more wind from the sail!

1. Less kicker

2. More kicker

1. Less outhaul

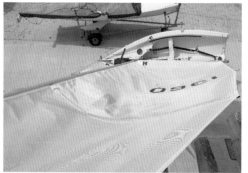

2. More outhaul

Outhaul tension

Outhaul has been pulled on which flattens the base of the sail. In super-light conditions (under 5 knots) you want the outhaul to be pulled fairly tight. If the sail has too much depth, the light wind simply won't have enough power to get over the bulge. When the wind is above 5 knots and you are still looking for more power, it's time to ease the outhaul to increase sail depth, but never more than about 3 or 4 fingers width from the boom. When you are overpowered, pull the outhaul right back to flatten the base of the mainsail and depower the rig.

Cunningham tension

Cunningham has been pulled on which pulls the centre of effort (the main area of depth) forwards and flattens the mainsail. Only pull Cunningham on when you are overpowered. The windier it gets, the more Cunningham tension is required since it is your principal tool for depowering the mainsail. However, make sure to let the kicker (vang) and Cunningham off downwind when it's windy, otherwise you run the risk of snapping the mast. Don't let the kicker (vang) off too much, which will make gybes and downwind stability difficult.

1. Less Cunningham

2. More Cunningham

Have you forgotten anything?

- Make sure all split rings and sharp bits are well covered in tape, so they won't come undone or put a rip in the spinnaker.
- Make sure the hull is fully drained with bungs and hatches securely tightened.
- Make sure the spinnaker is the correct way up, will launch outside the jib sheets and shrouds, and can be pulled all the way back into the chute.
- Make sure there is full luff tension on the jib with no sag on a reach.
- Make sure the ends of the spinnaker and jib sheets are securely tied together, and the mainsheet has a figure-of-eight to prevent it running out of the blocks.

SAILING UPWIND

Maximum leverage from the crew holding down full power in the mainsail and jib provides optimum performance in light to medium winds, with a dynamic series of roll tacks driving the boat directly upwind…

Maximum power for Force 2-3

The mainsail should be sheeted in the centreline of the cockpit, without too much outhaul tension so depth in the bottom of the sail produces plenty of power. Frances steers up towards the wind to keep height while sailing over small wind-blown waves, with Tom fully hiked as Frances concentrates on holding the RS200 bolt upright – the boat should not heel to windward, which would make it slip sideways and lose height. The crew is responsible for moving in and out to hold the boat flat in gusts and lulls. The helm tries to sit in a constant position, simply moving her shoulders in and out to react to puffs while reading the water ahead.

Holding the boat flat

Start to ease the mainsail as the boat isn't quite flat with crew and helm both hiking. To ensure the mainsail retains maximum power when you ease the sheet, take slack out of the kicker (vang) to keep leech tension. Crew and helm weight should be closer together with the crew right up near the thwart. This concentrates weight over the most buoyant part of the hull, with maximum leverage and minimal pitching moment.

ROLLING THROUGH A LIGHT WIND TACK

The roll tack is a dynamic movement accelerating the turn and giving a power-punch to the sail. Before tacking, discuss the turn with your crew. Check there is clear water to windward.

Frances lets the boat heel slightly to leeward and sheets in the mainsail to help the boat head up to wind. This avoids using too much rudder, which would act like a brake across the back of the boat.

1.

2.

Throwing weight back with one co-ordinated movement, Tom and Frances pull the boat on top of them. The exact moment to do this is when the jib starts to back. Keep steering into the tack, but don't use too much rudder.

Communication is required for crew and helm to hop across the boat at the same moment. The rudder must be pulled straight when the boat starts to come flat, otherwise it acts as a brake. Tom uncleats the jib on the old side and sheets in on the new side while crossing boat.

3.

Stay on the old side while posting the tiller extension beneath the boom to the new side, using a small push on the rudder to get the bows through the eye of the wind. The crew must keep tension on the old jib sheet until this is achieved. Do not cross the boat too early or you will stall the tack.

4.

Hop straight into the toe straps on the new side. Frances does not swap hands yet – she has to make sure the tiller stays straight while Tom makes sure the jib is correctly trimmed.

5.

6.

Frances and Tom both throw their weight out on new side to pump the boat flat in one smooth movement. Frances holds the tiller straight throughout the pump, squeezing in the mainsail as the hull drops down. It is the crew's job to move in if there is too much weight on the side. Beware of the boat turning to windward when you pump it flat.

Keep the rudder straight and do not attempt to swap hands until the boat has settled on the new tack.

7.

Jib Trim

- Leeward side telltales should be streaming back. Windward side telltales should be starting to lift, with the top telltale lifting first.

- The narrower the slot, the more powerful the airflow over the leeward side of the mainsail. If the boat is hit by a strong gust, ease the jib sheet to open the slot and reduce airflow.

SAILING DOWNWIND

Heating it up with an asymmetric spinnaker is all about heading up to build power in the kite and then bearing away on increased apparent wind, letting the boat accelerate and sail at full speed, with a series of gybes leading directly downwind…

Full bore in Force 3

- In a Force 3 gust the mainsail is eased a long way off the centreline for asymmetric spinnaker sailing.

- The crew are both flat out on the side, getting as much height as possible to build power, whilst keeping the RS200 almost flat for optimum speed and control.

- If the boat heels further, Frances will start to get weather helm as the boat wants to head up constantly and fine control will be lost.

- As the wind increases you build up apparent wind, so the mainsail needs to be sheeted in progressively tighter and the crew needs to move weight further back to keep the bows up at higher speed.

Making the most of the breeze

- As the wind decreases, Frances steers high to increase apparent wind and power up the spinnaker. Both crew move forward and close together over the maximum area of buoyancy, lifting the stern, pushing down the bows and extending waterline length. The Cunningham is eased right off and the outhaul is slack to provide maximum power and fullness in the mainsail, with a small amount of kicker (vang) to control leech tension with the mainsheet eased.

- If you are struggling to lay a mark on a fine reach with the spinnaker due to being overpowered, let the kicker (vang) all the way off and pull full Cunningham on. This will depower the mainsail and allow the helm to spill more wind, so you can sail higher without heeling.

GYBING

Light wind roll gybe

As with a roll tack, a roll gybe is a dynamic movement that gives a power-punch to the sail. Key issues are for the helm to stay on her feet during the gybe, using them to steer the boat by controlling weight distribution. Holding the tiller extension on the new side deck while steering also helps control the arc of the gybe.

1. In a light breeze, the helm does most of the work rolling the boat through the gybe. Frances rolls the boat at almost 45° to bear away into the gybe, then grabs the gybing strop to pull the boom across.

2. She keeps one foot on the leeward side of the cockpit to keep the roll on, controlling the angle of heel with her weight. It's vital for the helm to stay on her feet throughout the gybe.

3. Frances steps across the boat as the boom swings to the new side, letting go of the gybing strop and straightening the tiller, while hand-holding the mainsheet. Tom remains pretty much centred throughout the gybe, but can slide up if help is required to control the roll.

4. Frances moves her weight to windward and gives a pump on the mainsheet as the sail gybes across to the new side, popping the battens so they curve with the sail and helping to pump the boat flat. The tiller is held dead straight throughout this part of the gybe. Once the boat has settled on the new gybe, Frances swaps hands on mainsheet and tiller.

Gybing reach-to-reach

Get the boat sailing at full speed and check everything is clear to leeward before starting the gybe.

1.

Frances has pre-gybed the tiller extension and uses a slight roll to windward to steer the boat into the gybe, while reaching for the gybing line. Tom keeps the kite full with the old sheet, but has grabbed the new sheet and is ready to pull in after the gybe.

2.

Frances holds the tiller extension against the new deck to prevent over-steering. She pulls the boom across, using her feet to control the angle of heel and steering. Tom pulls the new kite sheet across, keeping tension on the old kite sheet to prevent a twist in the luff.

3.

Frances puts her weight on the new side to bring the boat flat, pumping the mainsheet as the boom swings across, still holding the tiller behind her back with a dead straight rudder to prevent the boat rounding up out of control. Tom concentrates on sheeting in and filling the kite.

4.

Once the boat is settled and flat, Frances swaps hands on mainsheet and jib. She pushes away the tiller to heat up the spinnaker and get the boat back up to speed, with Tom moving onto the side as the kite powers up.

5.

As always good communication saves the day!

6.

7 | Buying a Dinghy

Performance levels

Dinghy design is a compromise. At one extreme you can get sedate performance with maximum stability, making the boat as user-friendly as possible for novice sailors. At the other extreme you can get rocketship performance with minimum stability, making the boat highly demanding for experienced sailors. Cost is also a major compromise. Dinghies with low cost hull construction, such as rotomoulded plastic, are invariably heavier and more flexible than dinghies with more expensive fibreglass foam sandwich construction. More expensive dinghies also tend to provide more refined performance and handling, due to better sails with more sophisticated controls.

Big spinnaker + high aspect mainsail + lightweight hull construction = speed.

New or second-hand?

Dinghies are widely available second-hand, which makes it possible to save a considerable amount on buying new, with older dinghies on sale at a fraction of the price of the latest models. It is important to check the condition of the boat. The rig and fittings of any dinghy will cease to function properly with use and abuse, and may be costly to replace, particularly sails which will eventually stretch, delaminate or rip. Scratches and dings in the foils and hull should be checked carefully – they may be straightforward or impossible to make good. Older dinghies may have more severe structural problems, typically around the gunwale, mast base, centreboard case or rudder fittings. These kind of problems are removed if you buy new, with the added bonus of getting the latest kit with access to finance, support from the manufacturer and a guarantee. Best advice if you wish to buy second-hand is to research the type of boat carefully, find out what to look for and if possible get an expert to help with the final choice. The good news is that many members of sailing clubs know a lot about their boats, are keen to encourage newcomers and tend towards fairness and honesty when they sell. After all, dinghy sailing is a lifestyle and sport.

The Graduate is a typical traditional twin-crew racing class with mainsail and jib, but no spinnaker. This kind of design is ideal for tactical racing on lakes and reservoirs.

Racing or recreation?

Having mastered the basic techniques of dinghy sailing, you may feel it's time to seek greater challenges than simply sailing around for fun. Racing is a great way to improve boat handling, set personal targets, enjoy the thrill of sailing at close quarters and meet like-minded friends. Curiously, a racing dinghy does not have to be an expensive high performance sailing machine. The great majority of dinghies are suitable for racing, either as a one-design or in a handicap fleet. Relatively cheap and unsophisticated dinghies such as the Topper, Laser or RS Feva are among the most popular dinghies for both racing and recreation. Top level dinghies that provide extreme performance, such as the Olympic 49er skiff or foiling International Moth, have much more limited appeal because they are expensive to run, difficult to sail and require a lot of time and commitment.

The rotomoulded Topaz provides a low cost solution to buying a brand new boat.

8   The Beaufort Scale

Admiral Sir Francis Beaufort, who lived from 1774 to 1857, is widely credited with the invention of the Beaufort Scale in 1806 while serving on board HMS Woolwich. In times long before reliable anemometers, it was used to help sailors estimate wind strength by matching the appearance of the open sea against a list of careful descriptions. It seems likely that similar scales of wind force were in use many years before Admiral Beaufort was even born, but the immortal Admiral still gets all the credit! In modern times, the Beaufort Scale is still widely used for maritime weather forecasts and quoted by dinghy sailors and yachtsmen as the official gauge of the wind.

Force	Knots	Mph	Km/h	Description	On Land	At Sea
0	0-1	0	0	Calm	Smoke rises vertically	Like a mirror

No use for sailing. Wait on the beach and make sure your boat is perfectly prepared.

Force	Knots	Mph	Km/h	Description	On Land	At Sea
1	1-3	1-3	1-6	Light air	Wind direction indicated by smoke drift	Ripples on the water without foam crests

Not much use for sailing. Drifting on flat water, with the crew sitting right forward to lift the stern and the boat heeled to leeward to put some shape in the sails.

Force	Knots	Mph	Km/h	Description	On Land	At Sea
2	4-6	4-7	7-11	Light breeze	Wind felt on face and leaves begin to rustle	Small wavelets but crests do not break

Good for beginners. The boat will pick up a little speed and may heel slightly to leeward – enough for a dinghy crew to sit up on the windward side.

Force	Knots	Mph	Km/h	Description	On Land	At Sea
3	7-10	8-12	12-19	Gentle breeze	Wind extends light flags Leaves and twigs in constant motion	Large wavelets with a few white horses

The start of a good sailing breeze. Hike upwind to hold the boat upright with full power in the rig and potential to plane on a reach.

Force	Knots	Mph	Km/h	Description	On Land	At Sea
4	11-15	13-18	20-29	Moderate breeze	Dust and loose paper raised. Small branches are moved	Small waves with fairly frequent white horses

Perfect conditions for sailing. Dinghy crews will be fully extended, hiking or on the trapeze, depowering the mainsail upwind and planing fast offwind.

Force	Knots	Mph	Km/h	Description	On Land	At Sea
5	16-21	19-24	30-39	Fresh breeze	Smaller trees sway	Moderate waves with many white horses

Challenging conditions for dinghy sailing with very good technique required to handle the wind. Most boats will be well overpowered. Capsizes will be frequent.

Force	Knots	Mph	Km/h	Description	On Land	At Sea
6	22-27	25-31	40-50	Strong breeze	Large branches are swaying. Umbrellas are used with difficulty	Large waves start to form with white foam crests and some spray

You need to be extremely good to manage a dinghy in this much wind, though exciting sailing is possible in sheltered water with reliable safety back up.

Force	Knots	Mph	Km/h	Description	On Land	At Sea
7	28-33	32-38	51-62	Near gale	Inconvenience felt when walking against the wind with whole trees swaying around	Sea heaps up with white foam blown in streaks along the waves.

Too much wind for dinghy sailing – pure survival conditions!

9   Glossary

Apparent Wind Wind speed and direction when a boat is moving, as opposed to true wind when a boat is static.

Asymmetric A spinnaker with longer luff than leech, as opposed to a traditional spinnaker which has equal length sides. Also known as a 'gennaker' or 'kite'.

Back Wind rotating anti-clockwise, against the sun.

Backed A sail filled in the reverse direction. The jib 'backs' to help pull the bows round when tacking.

Balance Holding the boat upright and level.

Barber hauler Control to adjust horizontal sheeting angle of jib.

Bearing away Turning away from the wind.

Beaufort Scale Traditional wind speed indicator.

Blanketing During a spinnaker hoist or drop, the spinnaker is protected (blanketed) by the mainsail.

Burgee Small flag at the top of the mast.

Centreboard Main foil which swivels up and down inside case.

Chainplate Adjustable attachment between shroud and hull.

Chute Tubular chute which stores the spinnaker in the foredeck. Can be a cloth sock or solid chute built into the bows.

Clew Back corner of sail.

Cunningham Control line used to tension luff of mainsail, which bends the mast and flattens the sail.

Dacron® Woven sail material. Traditionally white in colour. Mainly used for jib and mainsail on lower cost dinghies.

Daggerboard Main foil which lifts vertically up and down.

Epoxy Top quality resin used with glassfibre and other woven materials to create strong and light laminate for dinghy hulls and decks. Other resins include polyester and vinylester.

Foam sandwich Hull construction using lightweight foam core between thin inner and outer laminates which are generally glass fibre, although materials such as carbon fibre may be used. Provides optimum balance of stiffness and light weight.

Foils Rudder blades, daggerboards and centreboards.

Foot Bottom of a sail.

Forestay Front wire which holds up the mast. Many dinghies incorporate forestay inside a wire jib luff.

Gnav Strut which pushes down on top of boom, providing same function as kicking strap.

Gradient Wind Wind due to weather systems, not local effects.

Gudgeons Brackets for rudder pintles attached to the transom.

Gybing Changing tacks with the wind behind.

Head Top of a sail.

Headboard Reinforced top of mainsail.

Header Wind shift taking you further from an upwind destination.

High 'Going high' or 'luffing' is sailing towards the wind.

Kicking Strap Rope or wire control used to pull down the boom. Also known as 'kicker' or 'vang'. Important for managing twist which bleeds off excess power from the leech of the mainsail. A Gnav has the same function.

Kite Euphemism for spinnaker.

Larks Foot Rope looped through itself. A double larks foot can be used to attach sheets securely to the clew of a jib or asymmetric spinnaker.

Leech Trailing edge of sail.

Leeward The direction in which the wind is blowing.

Leeward boat A boat downwind.

Leeway Being pushed sideways by the wind.

Lift Wind shift taking you closer to an upwind destination.

Low 'Going low' is sailing away from the wind.

Lowers Lower shrouds to control mast bend.

Luff Leading edge of sail.

Luffing Turning towards the wind.

Mast Rake Angle of mast from vertical.

Mast Ram Mechanism used to control lower bend in mast on some racing dinghies.

Mylar® Laminate material for mainsails and jibs. Very resistant to stretch under load, but less durable than traditional woven polyester.

Neap Tides Period of month when tidal range is smallest.

One Design A dinghy class in which all boats are exactly the same.

Outhaul Control for tensioning foot of the sail.

Pentex® Laminate material mainly used for mainsails.

Pinching Squeezing very close the the wind on a beat.

Pintles Steel pins for attaching rudder stock to gudgeons on the transom.

Planing Skimming over surface of water on bow wave. This provides a substantial boost in speed over displacement sailing through the water.

Pointing Pointing towards the wind while sailing fast on a beat.

Port Left.

Port Tack Sailing with the wind on the port side.

Pumping Moving the sheet rapidly in and out to power the sail.

Rip Stop Lightweight nylon for spinnakers.

Rocker Longitudinal curve in the hull shape. More rocker helps the boat turn faster, but a flatter hull is potentially faster in a straight line.

Roll Tack A rolling tack which fans the sails for increased drive.

Rotomoulding Manufacturing technique for producing low cost dinghy hulls in sturdy polyethylene plastic. Principal disadvantages are extra weight and lack of stiffness.

Shrouds Side wires which hold up the mast.

Slot Area of wind flowing between mainsail and jib.

Spreaders Horizontal struts to control lateral mast bend.

Spring Tides Period in month when tidal range is greatest.

Starboard Right.

Starboard Tack Sailing with the wind on the starboard side.

Tack Front corner of a sail.

Tacking Changing direction with the wind ahead.

Telltales Wool or plastic strips which show how air is flowing across the sails.

Tidal Range Difference between high and low water.

Transom Flat back at the stern.

Trapeze Wire for the crew to hang off suspended from the mast for greater leverage.

Traveller Slider which allows the mainsheet to be pulled to the windward side, in order to pull the boom onto the centreline in light winds.

Trim Fore and aft adjustment of crew weight in boat.

True Wind Wind speed and direction when a boat is stationary.

Twist The shape of the mainsail or jib when seen from astern. Twist in the top of the sail is used to reduce power upwind.

Veer The wind rotates clockwise or in the same direction as the sun.

VMG Velocity Made Good is true speed to a specific target. As an example, Dinghy A and Dinghy B have to reach the same target. Dinghy A runs directly downwind and sails the shortest possible distance, while Dinghy B gybes from reach-to-reach at higher speeds over a longer distance. Whichever dinghy reaches the target first has greater VMG.

Weather Helm A sailing dinghy has a tendency to steer upwind. Slight weather helm is normally desirable since it gives a more precise feel when holding the tiller.

Wind Bend Wind shift that increases as you sail into it.

Wind Shadow Sails affected by turbulence from other sails, boats or obstructions. Also known as 'dirty wind'.

Wind Shift A change in wind direction, which may necessitate a tack or gybe.

Windward The side the wind is blowing from.

Windward Boat A boat upwind.

10 Index

Organisations

www.rya.org.uk	Royal Yachting Association (RYA)
www.sailing.org	World Sailing

Weather

www.windguru.cz	Popular weather forecast website for sailing and windsurfing.
www.metoffice.gov.uk/weather/marine/inshore_forecast.html	Detailed forecast for inshore waters around the UK.
www.xcweather.co.uk	Designed for aircraft, but provides detailed information on forecast wind speed and direction across the UK.

www.rya.org.uk/go/join

LOVE DINGHY SAILING?

Then why not join the association that supports you?

Join the RYA today and benefit from

- Representing your interests and defending your rights of navigation
- Free class certification and discounts on sail numbers for members who race
- Personal advice and information on a wide range of dinghy sailing topics on UK waters
- Legal advice on buying and selling a boat and other boating related matters
- The latest news delivered to your door or inbox by RYA magazine and e-newsletters
- Boat show privileges including an exclusive free RYA members' lounge
- Annual RYA Dinghy show
- Discounts on a wide range of products and services

Get more from your boating; support the RYA

Want to know more?

Then call our friendly and helpful membership team on 02380 604 100 or email: member.services@rya.org.uk

The RYA... be part of it   www.rya.org.uk

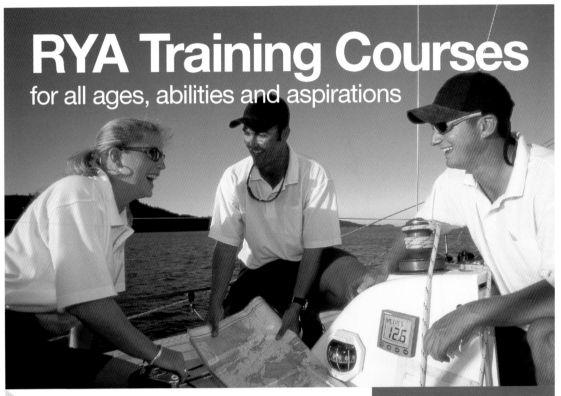

Notes